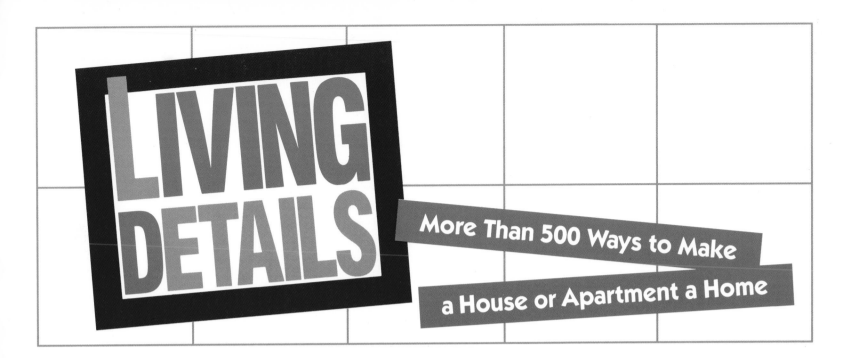

# LIVING DETAILS

## More Than 500 Ways to Make a House or Apartment a Home

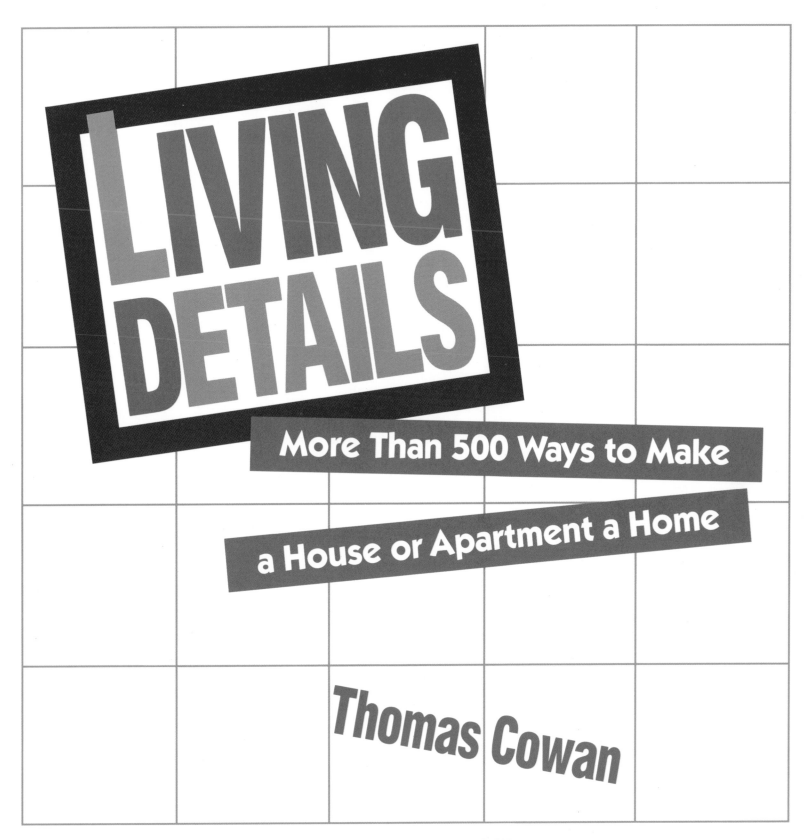

# LIVING DETAILS

## More Than 500 Ways to Make a House or Apartment a Home

### Thomas Cowan

WHITNEY LIBRARY OF DESIGN
An imprint of Watson-Guptill Publications
New York

A QUARTO BOOK

Copyright © 1986 by Quarto Marketing Ltd.

First published 1986 in the United States by Whitney Library of Design,
an imprint of Watson-Guptill Publications, a division of Billboard Publications, Inc.,
1515 Broadway, New York, N.Y. 10036.

Library of Congress Catalog Number: 85-041109

ISBN: 0-8230-7342-4

*LIVING DETAILS: More Than 500 Ways to Make a House or Apartment a Home*
was prepared and produced by
Quarto Marketing Ltd.
15 West 26th Street
New York, N.Y. 10010

Editor: Karla Olson
Art Director/Designer: Mary Moriarty
Photo Researcher: Susan M. Duane
Illustrations: Sharon L. Squibb
Production Manager: Karen L. Greenberg

Typeset by BPE Graphics, Inc.
Color separations by South Seas Graphic Art Company
Printed and bound in Hong Kong by Leefung-Asco Printers Ltd.

First Printing, 1986
1  2  3  4  5  6  7  8  9/91  90  89  88  87  86

# DEDICATION

To my sisters: Gail, Mary, and Margie

# ACKNOWLEDGMENTS

I'm indebted to all the kind salespeople who offered me their assistance, even after they discovered I was only shopping for ideas. And to Karla Olson, whose keen editorial eye for detail pulled this book together.

# CONTENTS

INTRODUCTION

SECTION ONE

## THE BASIC CHALLENGES

# INTRODUCTION

**D**omestic details, the personalized elements of organization, structure, and decoration that make a living space become a home, are many and varied. For people just starting out on their own, living in their first apartment or house, making sure that all these details of homemaking meet their particular needs and desires can seem an almost insurmountable task. There is so much to plan, so many things to acquire, so much to pay for, so many things to fix or alter so they accommodate a personal lifestyle. To add complication, there is the certainty that this home is temporary, that they may not live where they are for more than two years, or that these first alterations are expedient measures until more extensive renovations can be made. It's easy to look at people who have been settled for five, ten, or more years and envy the

countless odds and ends they have, the individualized comforts and luxuries, and the know-how they have to put it all together.

*Living Details* is a resource book for people who plan to live only temporarily in their present homes, for people who, for financial reasons, must wait to completely redecorate their homes, and for designers who are asked to decorate a temporary or first home. In these cases, homeowners or renters are unable or unwilling to invest large amounts of money, time, or effort in home renovations, and yet are looking for attractive ways to organize and personalize their surroundings.

For people in such situations, certain questions concerning money, time, use, and ownership have greater importance than they do for those who have bought a home in which they plan to

live for a considerable number of years. While everyone considers these four factors before making purchases or beginning home improvement projects, mobile young professionals, people just starting out, and designers creating a home environment for these people, must take into account the transient quality of their lives. For them cost, time and effort, the amount of use a purchased item or an entire project will get, and the all important question of portability—can you take it with you?—become the critieria by which decisions are made.

In the following chapters you will find ways to make your present dwelling comfortable and attractive without having to invest more time and money in it than you think is reasonable, given the length of time you intend to stay there. You'll also find ideas for furnish-

Pillows in contrasting colors, textures, sizes, and shapes and a casual window treatment that allows ever-shifting patterns of sunlight work together to enliven an informal seating area (facing page). Why not let your temporary attitude dictate the interior design of your home? Here, tired furnishings are given new spirit and lift with casual coverings, and a cardboard box table and unadorned windows focus directly but with flair on your transitory state-of-mind (above).

ings you can take with you. The ease of transporting an item to a new location is of primary concern when it is costly or when it is an item that you'll want to keep with you over the years, such as a major piece of furniture.

No one wants to pay for improvements to someone else's property. If you rent, you must carefully consider every home improvement project that requires permanent changes in the structure. It doesn't make financial sense to panel a living room if you can't take the paneling with you. Nor would you build a sauna in an extra apartment closet, even if the owner approved of it.

The same is true of time. Many young working people choose to rent precisely so they won't have to spend time on household maintenance. Their priorities place career and social experience ahead of tinkering around the house. Or they have bought a house from which they commute to work every day and they usually don't have the time and energy to put into extensive improvement projects when they get home at night. It's important then to tackle only those projects that can reasonably be finished on weekends or in the evenings, with a minimum of inconvenience. The projects described here can be completed leisurely in your spare time and will not disrupt your living space for more than a few days.

Another important consideration, especially in rented space, is the amount of use a purchase or a project will get. If you plan to live in the present dwelling for a limited time, it may not be in your best interests to put time and money into something that you will not use very often. It may not be necessary, for example, to buy an air-conditioner if you live in a relatively mild climate that has only a few really hot weeks each summer. Similarly, it may not be wise to

*Butcher-block-topped drawer modules form a kitchen island here, but can be recombined for other storage purposes (facing page). Metal stairstep shelves make nice lightweight and multifunctional display units (above). These streamlined desk chairs are sophisticated enough to serve as independent armchairs, and their color is bold enough to stand out in a room of any size (right).*

arrange elaborate guest accommodations unless you'll be having enough guests to make the accommodations worthwhile. Makeshift beds or beds that can serve double duty as couches or daybeds would be the wisest choice.

Finally, the question of ownership underlies many purchases for renters and those who have bought a home as an investment. If possible, buy items that can be taken with you when you move. Avoid home improvements that will benefit the next tenant or that you will regret leaving behind for the next owner. Instead, buy furniture and appliances with an eye to the next location, in styles and models that are adaptable and flexible.

## DECORATE SLOWLY

When it comes to decorating, the best advice for people who rent their living space is to go slowly. Start with the basics—cleaning, painting, and organizing. Don't try to renovate all at once. Get used to the place you live in by living in it for a few weeks. Let ideas and decorating schemes germinate. Often the details will occur to you at odd moments of the day or while you're visiting someone. You may be inspired by what you see in magazines or department store displays. Ideas grow

upon ideas. Don't jump at the first decorating plan that occurs to you.

Remember that you can always find bargains and sales. If you buy an expensive item immediately, you may be sorry when you see a similar piece at a reduced price a month later. Friends and relatives often have furniture or decorative items that they will give you or let you borrow for your new home.

Taste and trends change. Don't buy faddish items unless you are willing to live with them when they are considered passé or unless you plan on replacing them every season or two as new fads take their place. What you may think is just the right piece for a living room or bedroom today may be

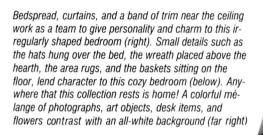

Bedspread, curtains, and a band of trim near the ceiling work as a team to give personality and charm to this irregularly shaped bedroom (right). Small details such as the hats hung over the bed, the wreath placed above the hearth, the area rugs, and the baskets sitting on the floor, lend character to this cozy bedroom (below). Anywhere that this collection rests is home! A colorful mélange of photographs, art objects, desk items, and flowers contrast with an all-white background (far right)

out of date in six months. A more traditional style, with simple lines, makes a piece of furniture adaptable for future living situations. Since you live with two uncertainties—where you'll live next and what styles you'll want to live with in the years to come—it's best to play it safe when making expensive purchases and buy styles that have proved to be enduring.

People in temporary living spaces don't have to decorate so that every room has a "finished" look. Nor does a room have to be decorated in one particular style. Home decorating for most people (even when they own their own homes) is an ongoing process. If you go slowly, you may learn that you can live without something you thought was of prime importance when you first moved in. You may discover that friends and guests don't even notice a wall or corner that you think looks empty. To them it may just look "minimalist." Make acquisitions and alterations one at a time and let each suggest to you the next step after you live with it and get to know it. You'll save money in the long run, make wiser and more careful decorating decisions, and may discover when it comes time to move that your "old" apartment or home really did look great. You can use the best ideas again in your new home, while leaving behind those that did not work.

Since you're planning to move or to do more extensive redecorating eventually anyway, let the ongoing decorating of your home become a metaphor for the condition of your life right now. In other words, if you plan to stay mobile for the next few years, forego decorating your apartment as if it were meant to last forever, but continue to make improvements every now and then and keep the look changing. A "finished" look has a "rooted" look, and since you don't intend to put down

roots just yet, let your home be a personal statement of your flexibility and mobility. Determine what you buy and what you change by what you personally find comfortable and aesthetically pleasing and what fits your budget and lifestyle.

## SHOP AROUND

Even when you are furnishing temporary living quarters, the advice of an interior designer can be helpful, as can ideas gleaned from design books, magazines, and show rooms. And window shopping as a kind of hobby will put you in a good position for making the wisest choices later on. If you can't afford to buy from expensive department stores and furniture shops, use their catalogs for ideas instead. What you see advertised at the upper end of the price range may be available at more modest prices during sales. You can also learn what high-quality features to look for when you shop. If you know what to look for and are very lucky, you may find sturdy pieces in second-hand stores, flea markets, and at garage sales. Follow the local auctions and want ads, too. If you don't know what's going on where you live because you just moved into the area, pick up the local shopper's guide. Also check in the yellow pages for nearby hardware and lumber stores, which may carry a wide range of housewares at more reasonable prices than the specialty boutiques and department stores.

The first important step before you even begin to shop is to measure your rooms carefully. Use graph paper and draw a scale model of each room, let-

*The clean, simple design of the flair arm sofas, the tub chairs, the cocktail table, and the wall units makes each element in this room highly adaptable to a variety of floor plans (right). Large plants—or small trees—complement any decorative scheme. Planters in different sizes lend themselves to many arrangements and uses (below).*

ting one square equal one foot. You might even cut out cardboard templates for furniture you now have (or are considering buying) and move them around on the grid to see how they will fit. Sales people complain about time lost dealing with customers who haven't the slightest idea how long a wall is or what the square-foot area of a particular room is when they try to buy furniture. Even closet space should be carefully measured before you look for shelving or closet organizers.

Use your scale drawing to determine traffic patterns. When people walk through rooms, they ordinarily take the shortest route, but if you want the traffic to flow in certain directions, you can encourage it by arranging furniture or dividers in a particular way.

When you do go shopping, take a tape measure and a notebook with you for comparison shopping. It's also a good idea to carry samples of fabric, paint, wallpaper or anything else you are matching since color often looks different in store windows and under the bright lights of display rooms. Size also can be misleading. Most furniture looks smaller in a store or a warehouse than it will look when you get it into your home.

As part of your buying strategy, develop the attitude of "no impulse buying" unless it is an item that you have been planning to get for some time and just didn't happen to be looking for specifically that day. Too often home furnishings bought on the spur of the moment look just right in the store window or show room, but all wrong once you get them home. They are usually items you never considered buying in the first place until you saw them so seductively displayed.

Well-displayed collections can set off a room's best features. A gallery of old photographs highlights the intriguing plaster finish of the wall on which they hang, while appropriately framing an antique washstand (above). A vast array of seashells complements a scheme of tawny hues and natural textures (right).

## THE BEST BUY

If you can't afford to buy many expensive pieces of furniture right away and the thought of living with only cheap or second-hand furniture depresses you, decide on one good piece that you can reasonably afford. Select something that will have lasting appeal and a style that will fit into a room no matter where you move next. A room can look very nice if it has one good piece of furniture and is finished off with less-expensive pieces, such as a new attractive media center in a room of older, used furniture.

There are no steadfast guidelines for judging quality in furniture, since each manufacturer has its own production techniques and builds assets and liabilities into furniture in its own way. In other words, there are trade-offs. Unless you are buying the very best furniture, you will probably have to sacrifice some qualities for the sake of other considerations. For example, a particular desk may be the right price and style but the drawers may not be adequately joined. A good buy is a particular piece of furniture that is strong where it will take the most wear, and weak in ways that will still allow it long life if you care for it and treat it properly.

Shop around and look at all styles, makes, and prices so that you become familiar with what makes furniture "top quality" and with the prices that good furniture commands. Do a lot of comparison shopping, from "expensive to cheap," from department stores that stock fine furniture to second-hand furniture shops. When you know good

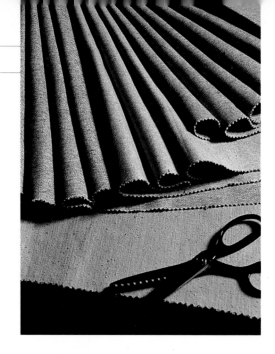

quality you'll be better able to recognize inferior pieces. What's more, you'll be able to spot superior pieces that turn up at flea markets or in the want ads.

## JUDGING QUALITY

Here are some general guidelines on what to look for when you inspect furniture, so you'll know what to sacrifice and what to insist on.

When buying upholstered furniture, make sure the frame is solidly built so the piece doesn't wobble. If the legs are merely screwed into the frame, the piece is poorly constructed. Legs should be joined to the frame with interlocking pieces.

A chair or couch with many spring coils is better than one with fewer. If each coil is tied with an eight-way tie and each cord fastened to the frame, you have a tightly built chair in which the springs will not move around. A four-way tie will let the coils shift too much and the seat will become lumpy.

Fabric on upholstered furniture is either natural (cotton, wool, linen, silk, leather) or man-made (nylon, polyester, rayon, vinyl). Whichever material you buy, the tighter the weave, the more longlasting it will be. Loose weaves wear out quickly, especially with hard use. On the other hand, if the piece is primarily for show and will get little use, a looser weave will probably hold up. Man-made fabrics have certain advantages over fabrics that are one-hundred percent natural: they are more durable, fade less, and resist soiling. Spots and stains come out of man-made fabrics more easily than from natural materials.

*Slipcovers and drapes fashioned by skilled hands from quality fabrics will camouflage a multitude of sins (right). The tall standing mirror and dark-stained bureau, both in bamboo, dictate the interior design of this room. An assortment of airy patterns in rich pastels cover every part of the room and fulfill the Victorian feel of the furniture. Darker, heavier colors and designs would overwhelm this little room (below).*

"Case goods" (an industry term that means un-upholstered furniture, such as tables, desks, chests, and cabinets) are either made of solid wood or are veneer, which is material made by bonding layers of wood to each other with a strong adhesive. In veneer construction, the center piece is thicker than the top and bottom pieces that are bonded to each side of it, and the most attractive grain is put on the exterior surface. Most furniture built today is veneer and is more durable than solid wood because of its layered construction. It is also considerably cheaper than solid-wood furniture. There are various grades of veneer, just as there are grades of solid wood, so comparison shopping and talking to sales people will help you to identify and evaluate various veneers.

Case goods are joined at the corners in several ways. A mortise and tenon joint is best for fastening backs to chairs and legs to frames. Desk drawers usually have a dovetail joining. This method, as well as the double dowel method, indicates good construction. Avoid furniture with butt joints, since they are the weakest type of joining.

When you judge the quality of case goods, inspect the back panels: They should be inset and screwed in place, not merely tacked on flush to the frame. Good-quality pieces are sanded and finished to match the exposed surfaces.

Drawers should have only a quarter-inch of play when moved from side to side. All four corners should be joined with dovetail joints.

The doors of a cabinet should not sag on their hinges when you open them and apply a little pressure. They should not swing shut when opened or

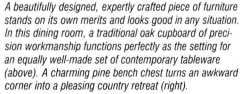

*A beautifully designed, expertly crafted piece of furniture stands on its own merits and looks good in any situation. In this dining room, a traditional oak cupboard of precision workmanship functions perfectly as the setting for an equally well-made set of contemporary tableware (above). A charming pine bench chest turns an awkward corner into a pleasing country retreat (right).*

pop open by themselves when the piece is bumped or jostled. Be sure all knobs, hinges, handles, and pulls are fastened securely or can be easily repaired or replaced if they aren't.

You may intend to buy a piece of used furniture you can refinish later. If not, be sure to check the finish carefully. It should be hard and smooth, not crazed with cracks across the wood grain. A finish that already looks crazed will only become more so. The finish may be of paint, lacquer, polyurethane,

synthetic varnish, vinyl sheets, or some other material. Each has its advantages and disadvantages. Ask sales people about a piece of furniture in terms of the use it will get and the atmospheric conditions to which it will be exposed, such as harsh sunlight, dry heat, and high humidity. The best finishes are sprayed on evenly, not dipped, and then covered with sealers and glazes. If you can see dark and light spots or gradations in the finish, it means the stain was not applied evenly.

## COLOR CHOICES

Color is really the key detail to decorating any room. It is the great unifier that pulls everything together and sets the mood. The colors on the warmer end of the spectrum—the reds and oranges—are hot and express happy, outgoing, friendly, sociable moods. The cooler colors—blue, green, violet—are

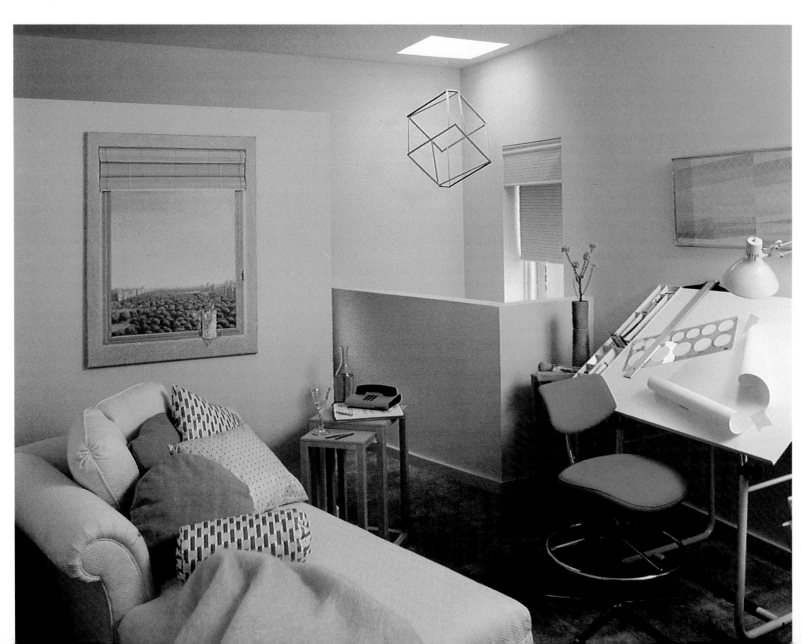

*Bright yellow walls and pastel accents make this room look bigger and brighter. The* tromp l'oeil *painting of a window and landscape add depth and freedom to the tiny confines (facing page).Flora abounds in this pleasant living room: in the plants and cut flowers, in the painting, in the matching prints of the window shade and table-cloth, and in the design of the sofa upholstery. This type of thematically consistent decor can pull together a roomful of disparate or lackluster furniture styles (above). A rich profusion of patterns and colors can either dazzle or frazzle the senses. The trick is to stress one particular color in the total ensemble, ideally the dominant color. Here, the same shade of red leaps out of each patterned item (right).*

more introspective, reclusive, quiet, and calm. Like the moods they express, warm and cool colors are changeable, shifting with the time of day and the amount and quality of light. The earth tones—brown, black, beige, deep greens, and russets—express a constant quality. They seem eternal, stable, and make an unchanging background for other, more variable, color moods.

When decorating a room with a basic pattern, such as in wallcovering, curtains, or bedspread, keep in mind that the dominant color in the pattern is the one that is most appropriate for the large areas of the rooms—the walls, floor, and ceiling. Use the next-brightest color in the pattern for the large furnishings and window treatments, such as shades, curtains, drapes, blinds, or even the casements themselves. Use the most striking color in the pattern in key accessories and other decorative items, to create a strong accent.

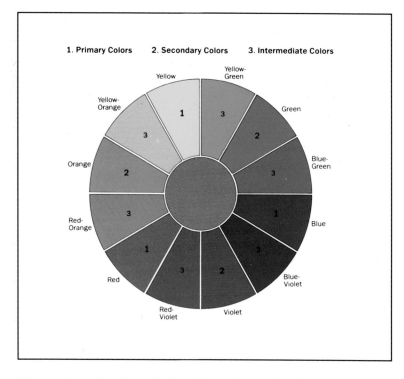

*Primary colors, such as blue and yellow, mix to make secondary colors, such as green. Intermediate, or tertiary, colors result from mixing primary and secondary colors. Generally, secondary with intermediate colors make the most pleasing combinations (above). If one primary color dominates most of your decor, it is best to restrict the rest of the decor to neutralizing blacks and whites. In this living room, dramatic red couches deserve to steal the color scheme (right).*

Color and pattern can be manipulated to create the illusion of space, both to enlarge it and reduce it. Bright colors, and the more passive pastels that seem to recede from the foreground, tend to make a room look larger. Darker, more aggressive colors make a room seem to shrink, creating a cozy, more intimate space. The same is true of patterns. Busy, tight, complex patterns make a room appear smaller, while quiet, open, simple patterns create the impression that the room is larger than it actually is.

Use color, too, to camouflage unwanted or awkward features. Pipes, unused doors, awkward fireplaces, or window frames that are painted the same color as the surrounding surfaces tend to disappear. Their visual impact can be minimized by "painting them out" or painting them a dark color causes them to visually recede from the brighter colors of the room.

Understanding a few principles of color can start you on your way to changing the look and atmosphere of an entire room. First, remember the three primary colors: red, blue, and yellow. All other colors are made from these three and have some of these in them. The secondary colors are those that are produced by directly mixing any two of the primaries, such as green from blue and yellow, or purple from red and blue. Tertiary colors are pro-

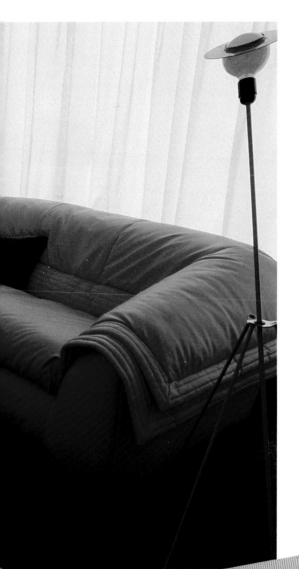

*The earthy tones of the wood, tile, and plaster work in this home are superbly complemented by the rich blue and red accents. Small touches in these colors, such as the red plate on the mantle and the blue in the painting on the wall, have immense visual impact against the neutral background (above). A primarily white color scheme comes alive with royal blue accents (below).*

duced by mixing a primary color with the nearest secondary color; for example, mixing the secondary color orange (red and yellow) with red to get reddish orange. Secondary and tertiary colors make harmonious combinations. Green and a blue-green, for example, would create diversity in the color scheme of a room without suggesting a clash. The combination would keep the mood of the room within a calming, narrow range.

Complementary colors, on the other hand, are opposites. Pair any color with one that is most unlike it, such as blue and orange, and you have a different kind of color scheme, one that is busy, invigorating, and alive. Often a color's complementary mate makes a good trim or accent to brighten a room. Keep this in mind when buying such accessories as clocks, book ends, ash trays, picture frames, telephones, and food containers.

Neutral colors are the blacks, browns, whites, tans, and grays. They provide a neutral surrounding for colorful furnishings, blend in with other colors and, when used as trim, can highlight the dominant color.

Even long-time homeowners can become swamped in the "living details" that make up their domestic lifestyles. But for the person living in a temporary space or a first home, there are truly unique challenges. Time, money, use, and ownership must be constantly considered when making major renovations or buying expensive pieces of furniture. But the challenge is what can make life in even the most ordinary space interesting and exciting. The creative solutions that you or your designer come up with, even when they are only temporary, will establish the ground rules and design guidelines that you'll rely on when you finally own your permanent home.

# THE BASIC CHALLENGES

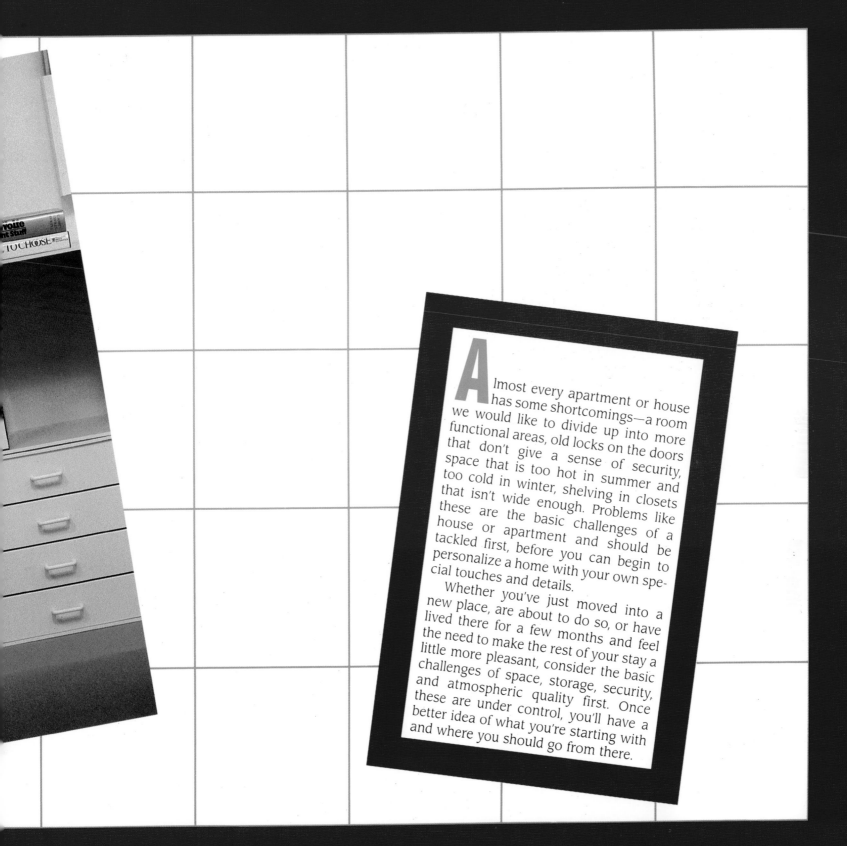

**A**lmost every apartment or house has some shortcomings—a room we would like to divide up into more functional areas, old locks on the doors that don't give a sense of security, space that is too hot in summer and too cold in winter, shelving in closets that isn't wide enough. Problems like these are the basic challenges of a house or apartment and should be tackled first, before you can begin to personalize a home with your own special touches and details.

Whether you've just moved into a new place, are about to do so, or have lived there for a few months and feel the need to make the rest of your stay a little more pleasant, consider the basic challenges of space, storage, security, and atmospheric quality first. Once these are under control, you'll have a better idea of what you're starting with and where you should go from there.

# CRAMPED QUARTERS

## STRATEGIC SLEEPING ARRANGEMENTS

If you find yourself in a home too small for even the necessities of life, your first strategy should be to double up on furniture wherever you can. Today's technology and design options have created a wide range of furniture with dual, triple, and even multiple functions. Such multi-purpose furniture is competitively priced when compared with the single-purpose pieces it replaces. Multi-purpose furniture can solve the problem of limited space in your present home, and can also be taken with you later on, still useful in one or more capacities.

The daybed, sofa bed, or hide-a-bed has been around for a long time, but the latest improvements have turned the combination couch and bed into a real piece of luxury furniture, one that actually does "hide" the bed. Even traditional convertible beds have been designed to look more like true couches during the day and have been structurally improved to provide comfortable beds at night. In many models, the metal frame that often could be felt through the lightweight mattress is now less obtrusive.

Some hide-a-beds and daybeds are built completely of solid foam, including both the sleeping-bed base and the contoured bolsters with arms that turn it into a couch. These are solid and comfortable. Most have covers that can be replaced if you change your decor or move to a new home. One model folds completely in half to create an almost square seat, and has a backrest made of overstuffed pillows.

When selecting a daybed, keep in mind that without some type of framing for a backrest or arms, you will have to use it against a wall to support the pillows. A convertible couch with a back and arms can be used in the middle of the room. Some of these come with a handsome wood frame, while others have metal tubular frames painted with a rubberized latex finish

Saving space can be a matter of cleverly designed rooms, cleverly designed furniture, or both. A loft built into a former walk-in closet neatly creates a bedroom atop a work/dining area. Strictly utilitarian furnishings contribute to the clean, unified look (facing page). A convertible sitting/sleeping unit doesn't have to be bulky or cumbersome. A colorful futon laid across an ingeniously flexible metal framework unfolds easily from an ultra-modern armchair to a comfortable bed (left). A finely proportioned sofa with a high, cushioned back and ample, split cushions doubles as a solid foam sleeping surface for two (below).

that can be enclosed in slipcovers for a softer look. These couches usually come with overstuffed pillows for lounging. Sizes range from easy-chair models that open into single beds to loveseats and full-length couches that sleep one or two people comfortably.

In recent years futons have been perfected. There are more styles, a wider selection of materials, and the construction is better. They, too, come with either wood or metal frames. Some models have multiple reclining positions, others only a few. Some can be conveniently turned into beds without moving them away from the wall; the mattress base swings forward as you lower it. Another attractive feature of futon furniture is that much of it is durable enough to use outdoors on a deck or patio. Buy a futon now for a

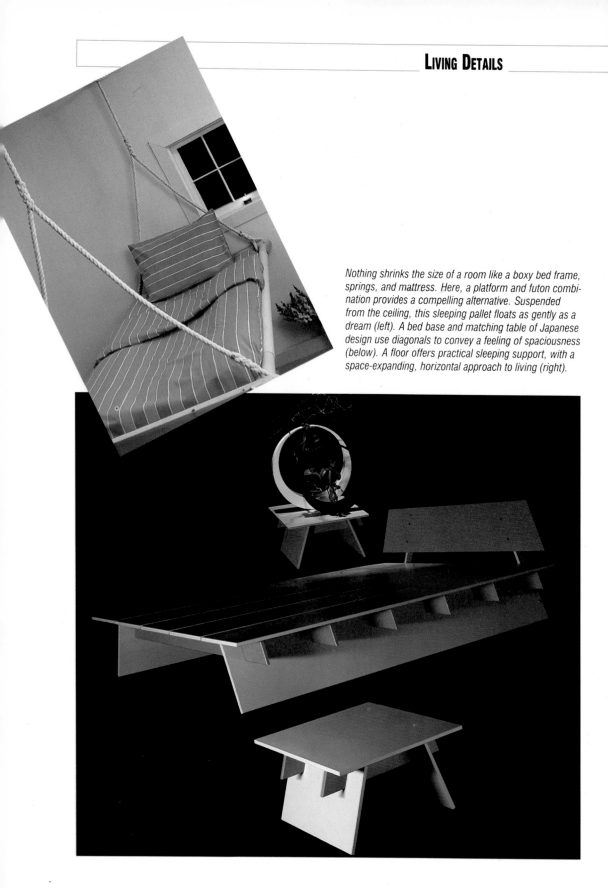

Nothing shrinks the size of a room like a boxy bed frame, springs, and mattress. Here, a platform and futon combination provides a compelling alternative. Suspended from the ceiling, this sleeping pallet floats as gently as a dream (left). A bed base and matching table of Japanese design use diagonals to convey a feeling of spaciousness (below). A floor offers practical sleeping support, with a space-expanding, horizontal approach to living (right).

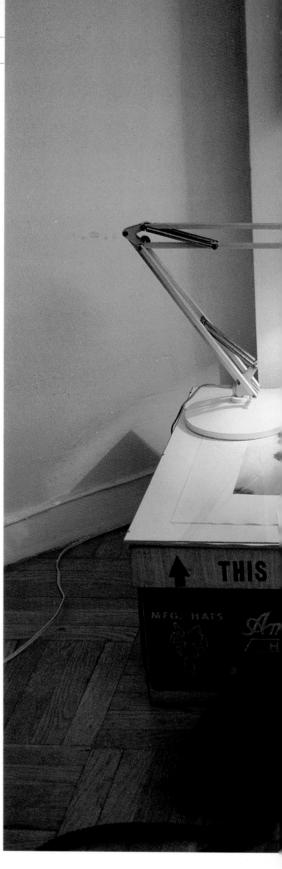

small apartment and later, when you own a home, you'll have a piece of patio or lawn furniture.

If you're wondering how to create sleeping space in a cramped apartment or where to put the bed in a large loft space, consider the Murphy bed of years ago. Murphy beds now come in handsome, freestanding, wood cases that extend only twelve inches out from the wall. When closed, they look like polished wooden cabinets or tall closets. Some come in a platform-bed design rather than in the sagging-wire-mesh design of yesteryear. Since they are freestanding, you can position them anywhere along a wall.

But for the most complete method of hiding beds, the latest modular wall systems provide total concealment. From the front they appear to be shelves, drawers, cabinets, even entertainment centers. The shelf system itself revolves out from the wall, and on the reverse side is a double bed, which is then pulled downward like a Murphy bed. Some models have weighted shelves that stay balanced and upright as the bed is lowered, like seats on a ferris wheel, so you don't even have to remove the objects on them. Glasses, dishware, even expensive art objects will stay put each night and morning, as the bed is raised or lowered and the wall revolved. The shelves come with optional doors, either glass or solid wood, that swing or slide open. The sections of the front can be designed to meet your needs. A full-length clothes closet can be transformed into shelves or drawer spaces as you need them. You can remove shelves or convert closet space to make room for a television or stereo system. Some models even have a pop-up table on the front.

One of the best features of such wall systems is that they are modular. Start with the simplest single-bed model and add enough sections to cover a thirty-foot wall. The system itself stands twenty-five inches from the wall. Two adjustable metal poles, designed like pole lamps but much more durable, brace the entire unit. By expanding the braces to fit snugly between the floor and ceiling, you can secure the wall system without driving nails or screws into the floor, walls, or ceiling.

An alternative to the wall system is the low counter system. It contains a pop-up table and a swing-down bed. A cabinet can be added to the top to create a hutch. You can use it against a wall or position it in a larger space as a room divider. The sleeping area is then located on one side, the dining or work table on the other.

## DOUBLE-DUTY TABLES

When you buy tables for small living spaces, look into the expandable models. The traditional design with optional middle leaves provides flexibility for mobile people who never know what size apartment or home they will be living in next. Without the leaves in place, some models are the size of card tables, but they open to almost dining hall proportions when fully extended. With this style, you can invest in a rather expensive table, knowing that it will fit almost any living situation that you find yourself in in the coming years. As a small table, it will fit an efficiency apartment; later, it could become your dining room table.

Besides those that open outward, there are tables that can be raised or lowered. When lowered, they make good coffee tables for living rooms.

*A mixture of the childlike and the sophisticated, a glass tabletop is balanced on four "popsicle sticks" to form the perfect dining table. Or the "sticks" can be splayed farther to the ideal height for a coffee table (facing page). This bedroom harbors a cornucopia of lounging and sleeping possibilities. A hammock, piled with pillows, provides a relaxing environment for daytime reading or snoozing. Bolsters on the bed offer a lounging alternative or an entirely separate sleeping surface when inverted and placed on the floor (right). Nesting tables are a handsome space-saver for the home entertainer. This unique trio of small, solid oak tables forms a compact cube that can serve as a plant stand or a coffee table (below).*

Raised, they become dining tables or work spaces. Another double-duty feature of some coffee tables is the storage space in or under them. Some models are as simple as a three-foot-square tabletop on a hinge over a two-foot-square box in which you can store such living-room items as coasters, games, books, and ashtrays. Still other models are designed to conceal chairs inside, so the chairs don't take up space when they're not needed.

## IMAGINATIVE LOUNGING

If you need more lounging space, consider the use of pillows and hammocks. Pillows can easily be made from fabric filled with pillow stuffing or shredded polyurethane bought at a dime store or variety store. Large pieces of foam rubber also work. Several solid foam pillows can be laid out for a guest bed and held together by a fitted sheet. If storing the pillows when they are not in use presents a problem, make them so they can be stacked.

A good hammock, even one wide enough for two people, can be securely bolted to wall studs to provide an area for reading, lounging, or watching television. The great feature of a hammock is that it can be put up without any thought to overall design or furniture placement, because its presence is temporary. A hammock near a bay window on a sunny day or in front of the fireplace on a wintry afternoon will make for good dozing and daydreaming. When you get up take the hammock down and stash it in a closet.

Imaginative shelving creates functional walls where space is tight or where separate spaces need to be defined. Large freestanding shelf units offer a ground-floor desk area plus concealing half-walls for an elevated sleeping space. A ladder provides access to high shelves as well as to the loft space (above). A custom-built wall incorporating bookcases, lamp supports, stylized cupboard space, and a reading shelf has an attractive three-dimensional effect that suggests it is the center of several different activities (left).

*The refrigerator too often looms large and awkward in the kitchen, where every square foot of space counts. The refrigerator, here has found its niche beneath a sealed-off stairway left behind when a house was converted into apartments. Its metallic whiteness is complemented by the cabinetry and the side of the stairs to give the entire area a crisp, geometric definition. The boldly colored stripes of the wall and ceiling camouflage the stair railing and enhance the effect (left). Surrounded by specially built cabinetry including a slide-in broom closet, this refrigerator seems to recede into a wall (right).*

## MAKING SPACES USEFUL

Another way to increase space is to figure out ways to use odd nooks and out-of-the-way corners. For example, if all you have available is a corner and you need desktop space, consider an L-shaped desk that bends around the corner. You can make one yourself, using a pair of two-drawer filing cabinets. Put one cabinet on each wall, cut an L-shaped top from heavy plywood (or have it cut at your local lumberyard), lay it on the filing cabinets, and support it with several cleats placed along the wall and in the corner.

Another seldom-used space is the area under a stairway. Here, too, you could construct a worktable or desktop for a home office. If the space is large enough, you might use it to store and use your hobby equipment, crafts supplies, or sewing materials. A daybed under a stairway makes a cozy nap and reading area for a small child. Build a platform bed with a simple foam mattress and plenty of pillows, and rig up a lamp so there is sufficient light for reading. Store games and children's books in drawers underneath. A bay window can be put to these same uses.

## DEFINING SPACE

A common problem with space is how to define it and delineate certain areas for certain purposes. Whether you are working with a large loft area or a small room that must serve several purposes, the key is to divide the floor plan as definitively, and interestingly, as possible. Furniture arrangements can be used to define space; group the tables, chairs, and sofas so they function as mini-rooms. If more than positioning and arrangement is needed to provide privacy or to visually cut off the rest of the room, a folding screen or shoji screen can be erected. A shoji screen will create a delicate but stable wall that can be removed and taken with you when you move. To spruce up an old folding screen, paint each panel a different color or cover the panels with wallpaper or fabric remnants.

For a less substantial room divider, consider suspending a piece of old lace sandwiched between two pieces of lucite that are screwed together at the corners. Use decorative chains to hang the panel from ceiling hooks. The lace will let both light and a sense of motion through, yet its semi-opaque quality will create a feeling of privacy. Instead of lace in lucite, use a panel of stained glass, which will define the space while casting colored light into the area.

Large house plants can also delineate an area of a room for a special purpose, as can the right lighting arrangement. (See Chapter Eight, "Decorative Touches," page 110.)

To create the illusion of a larger room, paint the walls a light, airy color, such as a pastel or off-white shade, or use wallpaper with a large, open pattern. To contract a large area, such as a

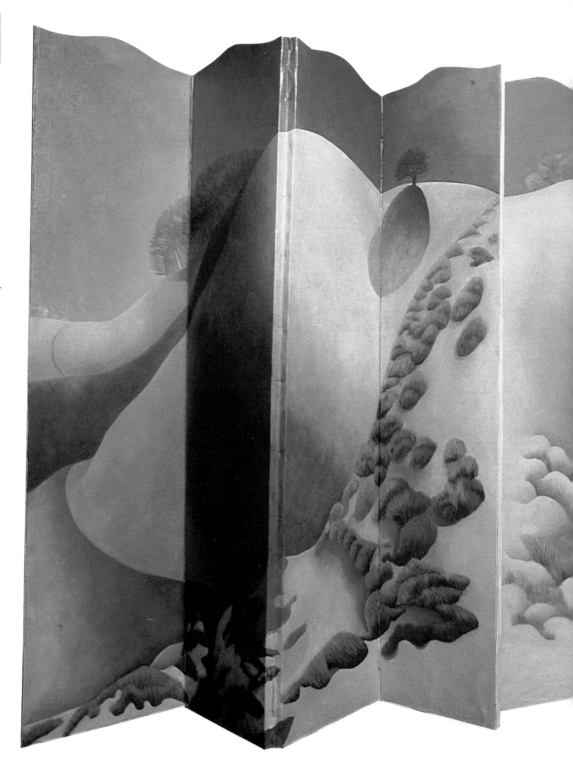

A hand-painted screen makes a visually dramatic room divider. It has a sculptural quality that offers a welcome contrast to walls and can be easily rearranged or removed as dictated by whim or occasion. Its stunning scene depicts an almost abstract mountainscape that gains additional relief through the different angles of the screen itself. The space beyond the screen is effectively cut off as if by a real mountain (left).

Translucent shoji panels give privacy and a subdued, restful atmosphere to this reading nook, where one could curl up to read or to take a refreshing midday nap. The simple rectangular pattern in the panels echoes the patterns of the book spines, bookcase shelves, cabinet moldings, and carpet and seat cushions (left). A freestanding storage wall turns one room into two. The size of the wall, which might have been overwhelming, is scaled down by embedded trim, rounded corners, cutaway sections, mirrored surfaces, and a thick coat of white, high-gloss lacquer. The wall is also balanced by its mirror image behind the bed (above).

corner of a loft or the end of a long, narrow room, and give it an identity of its own, paint its walls a darker color or paper them with a tighter, busier pattern. You can also create the illusion of depth in a room by hanging posters or prints that depict sweeping vistas or long, narrow streets. Let the artist's knowledge and use of perspective add

visual space and depth to your own, more limited, accommodation.

Nothing makes a room look more cramped than heavy furniture huddled together. While it's true that certain furniture is needed, and so you can't always get rid of it, you *can* buy furniture that is not cumbersome or heavy-looking. A glass tabletop on a dining

table and slimly structured chairs can almost make the setting disappear. Similarily, acrylic or glass-topped coffee tables and end tables in the living room will appear to take up less room. In general, any piece of furniture that has open areas in it or that is made of a see-through material will let more of the room be seen than will other styles.

*The freestanding position of every piece of furniture in this setting means infinite flexibility. You can tailor the space to accommodate any activity by simply moving the chairs and tables to where you need them (facing page). The mirrored tabletop, here, opens up what would otherwise be a cramped corner (above). This fascinating, Memphis-inspired table is stunning and very useful because of its glass top, which lets the sculptured base and hardwood floor take center stage (right).*

# SPARSE STORAGE

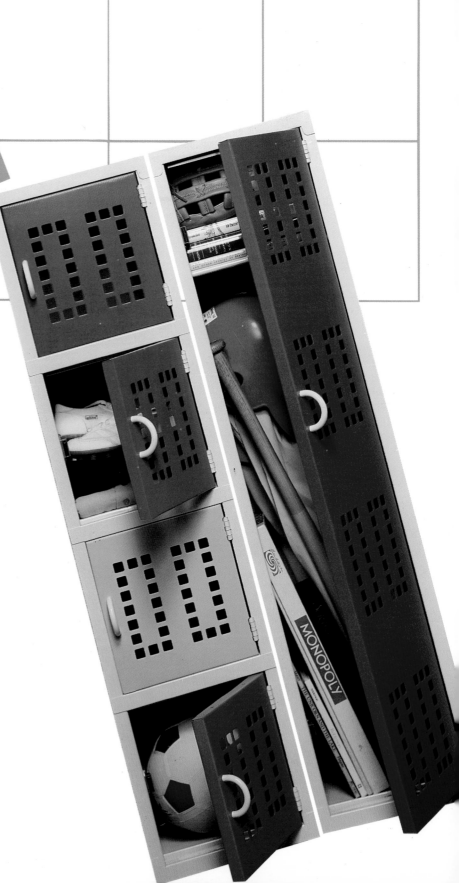

It doesn't matter how large a house or apartment is, lack of storage space always seems to be a problem. Eventually, possessions begin to stack up and it is challenging to try to find the right place to store them where they are out of the way but still accessible.

## CREATING
## USABLE
## SPACE

Built-in closets and shelves have been the traditional places for storage, but if your place seems to have been overlooked when they were handing them out, you may have to construct your own. You should also consider

*Increasing your closet space means adding new spaces as well as making more efficient use of the closets you have. What makes a more logical and practical storage complex for games and athletic equipment than playful, portable lockers with brightly colored doors (facing page)? A standard closet of one clothes rod with a single shelf above is remodeled to accommodate more items. Three smaller clothes rods—one above, another on the right—are installed across the sides of the closet. Modular shelving units in the center allow instant access to a wide variety of wardrobe articles (above).*

such nontraditional storage places as the space under beds, couches, and tables. There is a great variety of modular shelving and drawers available in a great many colors, materials, shapes, and sizes, all of which can provide extra, hidden storage.

Before obtaining modular storage space, make the most of the existing closets. Consider how you might enlarge the usable space, for usable space is the key concept. Short of tearing down walls, you can't really enlarge the actual space. But even closets that seem packed usually have dead space waiting to be shrewdly developed.

In older buildings, for example, the closet ceiling is usually quite high. Yet the shelf is normally at a level that the person of average height is able to reach. Unless you store large items on the shelf, the space above it is wasted. A second (or even third) shelf built over the original one lets you use that empty space. A shelf inside a closet doesn't have to be attractive. Simple one-inch by two-inch cleats nailed into the studs at either end of the closet, and on the back wall if the closet is long, will support a piece of plywood and create more shelving. Many people find two additional narrow shelves built in their closets perfect for storing books they want to keep but don't have room for in their bookcases.

Next, look in the lower regions of the closet. A clothes closet will often have wasted space from the bottom of the clothes down to the floor. Usually, shoes, a clothes hamper, and cardboard boxes filled with miscellaneous items are crammed into this area. You can create quite a bit more closet space for hanging clothes by installing another clothes rod beneath the top one.

Don't overlook the back of the closet door. Adding hooks or pegs will let you hang all kinds of things. Or install a

This closet has been transformed into a whole new type of room: a place to prepare for the outside world or to pull yourself together when you return home. The striped, pastel wall and ceiling covering; the white tile floor; and the sliding doors make the space look bigger than it is (left). This smart closet arrangement solves the problem of finding an out-of-the-way place for a hobby or a home office. Pull up a chair and everything needed is at an arm's reach (above). Odds and ends are gathered together in a usually wasted area beneath a stairway. Included among the matched shelving units is a fold-down desk, creating a personal work space away from the mainstream of household traffic (facing page).

pegboard so you can adjust the hooks to accommodate various items, such as ties, scarves, hats, belts, tennis rackets, and other sports equipment.

If you really need shelving rather than clothes rods, consider removing the original rod and building a closet full of shelves. They don't have to be perfectly trimmed and edged as though they are visible in a room. However, you might want to remove the door and leave the shelves exposed for easy access, or replace a swinging door with a folding door, a sliding screen, or a simple curtain.

One large closet could be turned into a single-purpose storage and work area, such as a sewing closet, small office, carpentry workshop, media center, home bar, or place to keep a baby's gear. Add shelves, a fold-down table or desk top, and drawers. Sometimes a small desk or chest of drawers that fits into the closet is all that is needed. You can keep supplies and tools in it, ready for when you want to work with them.

## ADDING MORE SHELVES

Attractive shelves can be built for any room. The usual scheme is to run them up the wall, but look around for other possibilities. Near the ceiling there is usually unused space. A three- or four-foot shelf extended out from the top of a door frame and attached to the

ceiling by decorative chains or one-inch by three-inch braces can be used for storing boxes or luggage. Similarly, a hallway can often accommodate a shelf near the ceiling, with several breaks in it for access. The effect is a lowered ceiling in the hall—the extra height is hardly missed. Ceiling lights in the breaks can produce a dramatic lighting effect and turn a dull hallway into more interesting space.

The corners of rooms and the space behind doors that always stand open are wasted spaces in many homes. Triangular shelves in corners can simulate a corner cupboard for dishware in a dining.area. Or use corner shelves for knick-knacks. If you have a door that usually stands open, look behind it and see how much space there is. Granted, it may be only four or five inches, but a rise of slender shelving may be just the thing for storing paperback books.

Wooden shelves can be trimmed in several ways. The simplest is to paint or varnish them to match other colors or wood tones in the room. But shelves can also be covered with fabric remnants. Pull the fabric tight and staple it on the underside of the shelf. Contact paper and scraps of wallpaper also make attractive covering.

Have you considered building closet and shelving space in one end of a room? It's not difficult. Decide how deep you want the storage area to be, and build shelves to fit within that space. Then hang a curtain rod or install sliding shoji panels to conceal the shelving. A cornice or valance can be added in front of a curtain rod. You might even make the enclosed area large enough for a bed and turn it into a sleeping nook. The space at either end of the bed can be used for shelves or chests. Use plywood paneling or folding screens to separate the storage areas from the sleeping space.

*Overhead space is often overlooked when household storage possibilities are being considered. In a porch area attached to the outside of the main building, a wide shelf provides a cache for plants and a basket, but also serves as a pleasing architectural element for the room as a whole. The shelf's strong horizontal line helps to reconcile the different heights of the two doorways. It also mediates between the pitched roof and the straight doorframes and provides a more dramatic entryway to the dining area beyond (below).*

A storage unit can serve as much more than just a functional necessity; it can be an aesthetically appealing component in the overall design scheme of a room as well. Here, a simple, wraparound shelf system creates a strong, satisfying border between the rich colors and varied patterns of the floor area and the minimalist treatment of the walls and windows. The vertical shelves of transparent plastic between the two windows displaying a collection of pottery do not distract from the lines of the shelves below. They also serve to ameliorate the impact of an exposed gas pipe (left). An odd-angled corner is successfully restructured with the help of a trim, well-balanced closet, shelf, and cupboard unit that blends smoothly into the walls around it (above).

The handsome teak furniture in this child's room has a look and style that the child will never outgrow. It also offers abundant storage space, so even the messiest child can be neat and well-organized with a minimum of fuss (above). These roomy square shelving modules can be fitted with drawers and doors to fulfill any and all storage needs (right).

As mentioned before, an often over-looked but useful space in a house or apartment is underneath the stairs. Usually this oddly angled nook is not large enough for a major use, but it can work as a place for storage. By adding shelves or a chest of drawers and enclosing it with curtains or sliding Japanese panels you have ample closet space for sporting equipment, tools, outdoor gear, luggage or even such utility items as a mop, broom, vacuum cleaner, and detergents.

## DECORATIVE STORAGE UNITS

One of the most recent developments for expanding storage space is the use of modular storage units. These drawers and bins can be stacked or grouped to create unique furnishings for odd corners and spaces. They can

*In small apartments you have to choose multipurpose storage units that are not visually overpowering. These handy units have a fluid shape and a special design that is attractive, nonobtrusive and voluminous. Their compact size and the transparency of the material they are made of help to keep the room looking as large as possible. Castors allow them to be rearranged easily, and a choice of tints enables you to select units that blend well with your other furnishings (right). The modular shelving units on the left wall of this room require no pins, screws, or clamps and can be rearranged into countless different types of storage systems. The stacking drawers beneath the window are also modular, durable, and quite easy to clean (below).*

be stacked high to form a chest of drawers, left as individual units for low end tables, or positioned to create a larger tabletop. They also make excellent room dividers. Some are sturdy enough to be covered with cushions or mattresses and used as couches or daybeds. They are produced in a variety of colors and materials to match other furnishings and decorating schemes. In effect, you can provide storage space and add furnishings to a room at the same time. One of the advantages of modular units is that you can buy as many as you need immediately and add to them as you accumulate more items. Your storage space grows along with your acquisitions.

In addition to storing items in modular units, many furniture companies now design beds, couches, and tables with hidden storage space. A platform bed with large roomy drawers beneath it and a deep storage bin in the headboard is a great space saver. Some couch models have storage areas beneath the cushion supports, and there are low coffee tables with hinged tops

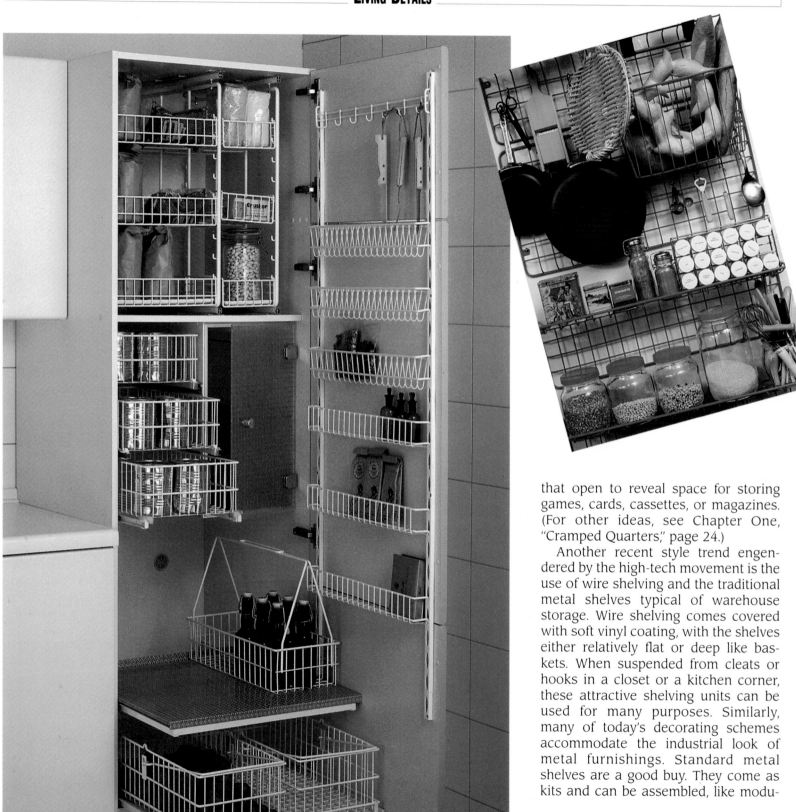

that open to reveal space for storing games, cards, cassettes, or magazines. (For other ideas, see Chapter One, "Cramped Quarters," page 24.)

Another recent style trend engendered by the high-tech movement is the use of wire shelving and the traditional metal shelves typical of warehouse storage. Wire shelving comes covered with soft vinyl coating, with the shelves either relatively flat or deep like baskets. When suspended from cleats or hooks in a closet or a kitchen corner, these attractive shelving units can be used for many purposes. Similarly, many of today's decorating schemes accommodate the industrial look of metal furnishings. Standard metal shelves are a good buy. They come as kits and can be assembled, like modular units, to provide as much shelving as is needed. You can either let items stand exposed, or put them in plastic bins or brightly colored cardboard boxes. If the raw metallic finish is too discordant for a room, the shelves are easy to spray-paint to match the walls or other furnishings.

Finding storage space is not always easy. It takes a careful examination and analysis of your apartment or home and a little imagination to discover that previously unnoticed spot waiting to be developed into an extra shelf, bin, or closet. Fortunately, however, once you've found the spot, it doesn't require advanced carpentry skills or a lot of money to make it useful.

*Vinyl-coated wire is one of the most versatile and space-saving storage elements around. This kitchen closet features baskets on hanging and sliding trays (facing page, left). Wire mesh racks and hooks support baskets, shelves, and utensils (facing page, right). A freestanding bookcase includes extra closet space at each end of the unit (above). A wire box makes an efficient but playful coatrack (right).*

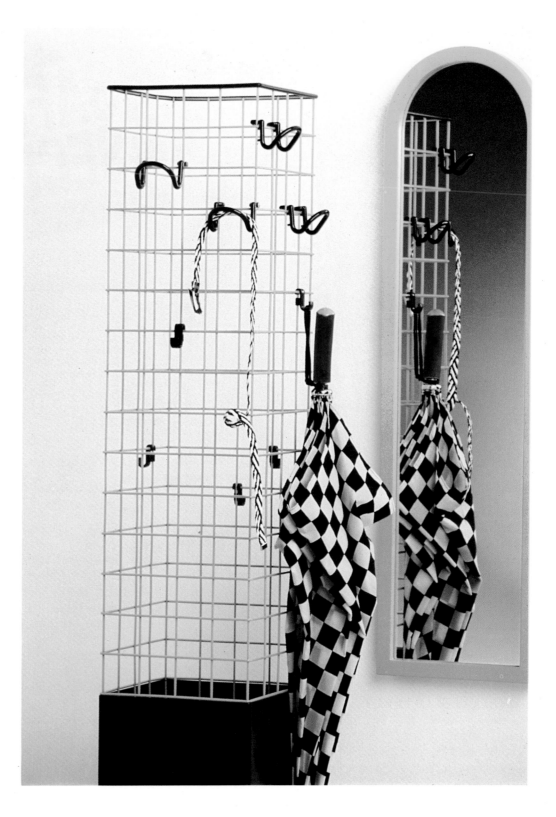

# SAFE AND SECURE

## THWARTING THE BURGLAR

In spite of the new technology in locks and alarm systems, professional burglars who want to break into your house or apartment will find a way to do so, because they keep informed about the counter-technology developed to outwit new security devices. Fortunately, not all thieves are professionals. Most breaking- and-entering is done by youthful vandals looking for easy money, for items to sell illegally, or just for kicks. While it's impossible to make your home or apartment completely burglar-proof, you can install security measures to outwit, slow down, or discourage many would-be burglars.

The three key factors that prevent successful burglaries are time, noise, and visibility. If your doors and windows are securely locked, a burglar will need more time to break in. In that added time, someone may notice, or the burglar may become nervous enough to give up. Similarly, if breaking through your security measures requires sawing, drilling, gouging, or shattering, the noise might alert neighbors or passersby. Visibility is also an important deterrent; no burglar wants to be watched. Trim bushes or trees near any windows, and install outdoor lighting to eliminate shadows that could conceal a burglar's approach.

## SECURING DOORS

Although no house is completely burglar-proof, there is much that can be done to make your home more burglar-resistant. First, consider exterior doors. Make sure the door frames are solid and securely attached to the wall studs. If you are moving into an older building, check to see if prior burglary attempts have left the frames chipped or weakened. You may have to replace them or attach metal jimmy plates around the exterior edges. A jimmy plate is excellent for any door that does not fit tightly in its frame.

Since you will not want to replace a mortise lock in a door that belongs to someone else, your best bet is to add a

A mortise lock with a deadbolt feature—the two more prominent prongs issuing from the lock face on the right—offers solid, basic outside door security (facing page). A professional household protection service usually consists of an alarm system that is triggered by an intruder breaking a circuit at any point of entry or setting off a motion detector (above). Outdoor floodlighting, especially around potentially concealing greenery, helps to discourage burglars and minimize accidents (right).

deadbolt rimlock. Unlike a mortise lock, which is built into the door itself, a rimlock is attached to the surface of the door. The deadbolt enters a strike box, which is attached to the surface of the frame rather than cut into the frame as with a mortise lock. The deadbolt does not have a spring-activated strike, so it can only be opened with a key. A double-cylinder deadbolt requires a key to activate it even from inside the house. Unlike single cylinder deadbolts, which are operated from inside the house by means of a knob, the double cylinder prevents a thief from breaking the glass in the door or kicking through a panel and reaching in to unlock the door.

Another good security feature is the vertical dropbolt, which, like a hook, catches in the metal strike box. Whereas a horizontal deadbolt can be pulled out of the strike box if the door is pried from the frame, the vertical drop-bolt catches on the strike box. The dropbolt is further protected by a metal casing, which prevents a burglar from sawing through it.

Many houses and apartments have sliding glass doors, which are extremely vulnerable. A Charlie bar, made of metal or wood and wedged between the sliding panel and the opposite frame, will slow a burglar down but will not prevent the door from being pried off the track with a screwdriver. Special patio locks, however, are easy to install and quite resistant to attack. Drill two bolt holes into the lower frame of the stationary panel near the sliding section and screw a metal strike plate over them. The door is secured by key-locking a metal wedge into the bolt hole. Its curved end butts the sliding section and prevents it from moving. This lock also makes it harder to jimmy the door off the track.

Install a peephole if your door doesn't already have one. Most apartment owners will not object if it is done properly. Simply drill a hole through the door and insert an inexpensive peephole bought at a hardware store.

The new design in keys is another feature worth investigating. Looking like futuristic devices from science fiction fantasies, these new keys are virtually impossible to duplicate. The Fichet, the Medeco, and the Sargent Keso, for example, employ various sides, angles, and grooves that are coded and so can't be duplicated. The locks they fit are also much more difficult to pick.

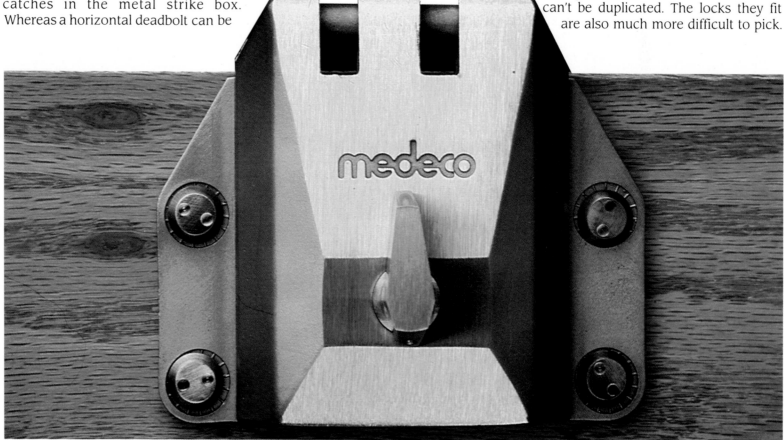

An eye-level peephole, seen here on the outside of the door, works together with a double deadbolt lock and a chain guard to provide three security checkpoints (above). An interlocking deadbolt, key operated outside and knob operated inside, is difficult for an intruder to force (facing page). An elegant lock and door handle set provides beauty, convenience, and security at an entryway (right).

## PROTECTING WINDOWS

Windows are a prime point of entry for many burglars, and many people make it all the easier for them by not locking their windows when they go out. The old-fashioned and virtually worthless butterfly locks on double-hung windows can be picked with a kitchen knife. There are improvements on this type of lock, however, that eliminate the crack between the two sashes. Some of them are key-operated.

A simple and inexpensive do-it-yourself method of securing double-hung windows is to drill holes in the window frame where they overlap or at the sides where they butt the sash. Don't drill all the way through the outside frame, or a burglar will be able to remove the bolts. Insert a strong, thick nail or bolt into the holes when you are away. Another set of holes drilled in the outside frame a few inches above the bottom holes will allow the window to be bolted open a bit.

A wedge lock for a double-hung window, similar to the patio lock for a sliding door, is key-operated and creates a good resistance. The strike plate is installed on the frame of the upper half, just above the lower window. To secure the window, the wedge is key-bolted into the strike. A second strike mounted a few inches above the other lets you lock the window open a few inches for ventilation.

Aluminum windows can be locked with a clamp lock that is fixed to the metal sash and removed when you want to open the window. Buy only key-operated locks; otherwise, a burglar can break the window and remove the lock. A handy feature of these locks is that they can be locked at any spot

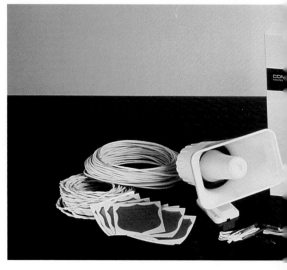

*An integrated household protection system provides the most effective security available. This one is wired to set off a loud alarm whenever an intruder breaks a circuit by forcing any point of entry. System decals attached to windows and doors frighten potential burglars away before they enter (right).*

on the sash allowing you to lock partially opened windows.

Another safety feature for windows is the metal grill that operates from the inside. The standard accordian grill, used for a window that opens onto a fire escape or one in street-level or top-floor apartment, folds up when you want to go out the window. Safety regulations issued by your local fire department may require that the grill be easy to unlock and remove from within so you can get out in an emergency. Some are key-operated; others pop out by means of a special maneuver only possible from inside the room. Most grills have a prisonlike quality to them, but some are more attractive than others. Even the most utilitarian model can be painted to match your interior decor. Be careful, however, not to paint an expandable grill so that it sticks.

## QUALITY PADLOCKS

Many people living in temporary quarters have to store some of their belongings in storage rooms or basement bins, and the easiest method of securing them is with a padlock. With so many padlocks on the market, it's good to know what to look for. Be sure the body of the lock—its case—is laminated, rather than wrought, steel. The thicker the case, the better. If corrosion may be a problem, buy one coated with corrosion protection. Brass is better than steel, and a shackle that is chrome- or nickel-plated will withstand moisture. Always check the shackle for the word "hardened," which means it is case-hardened to withstand bolt cutters and hacksaws. A double-locking

shackle has a groove on both the heel and the toe, thus securing both legs and making it harder to spring open. Never trust valuables to a warded padlock; a warded padlock is easy to detect by the shape of the key, which has identical notches on both sides. Instead, buy a pin-tumbler lock, which is much more difficult to pick and has a key that is much harder to duplicate.

## ALARM SYSTEMS

Security alarms for homes and apartments use the latest electronic wizardry to thwart thieves. If you're living in a rented dwelling, you probably won't want to install a hard-wired perimeter alarm system, which requires running permanent wires through the walls. But if you are in a new house, this investment early on might be worthwhile. In this system, magnet sensors are attached to doors and windows so that one half is on the movable part, the other fixed to the frame. When the door or window is closed and the alarm system turned on, a circuit of electricity runs from the sensors through the wires to the alarm box. When the door or window is opened, the circuit is broken and the alarm sounds. Even if the thief closes the door or window, a relay switch keeps the alarm running.

There is, however, a "wireless" version of this system, in which the sensors are wired to small transmitter boxes. These send alarm signals by radio waves to a centrally located control box that emits the alarm. The wiring involved does not require permanent installation in walls; there are only sim-

*A compact control unit for a household protection system allows you to set alarm mechanisms either on or off and alerts you, the police, and/or the fire department to any threatening situation (facing page). The Honeywell System 2000 protects windows against intruders, but allows you the flexibility to leave a window open when you choose (below).*

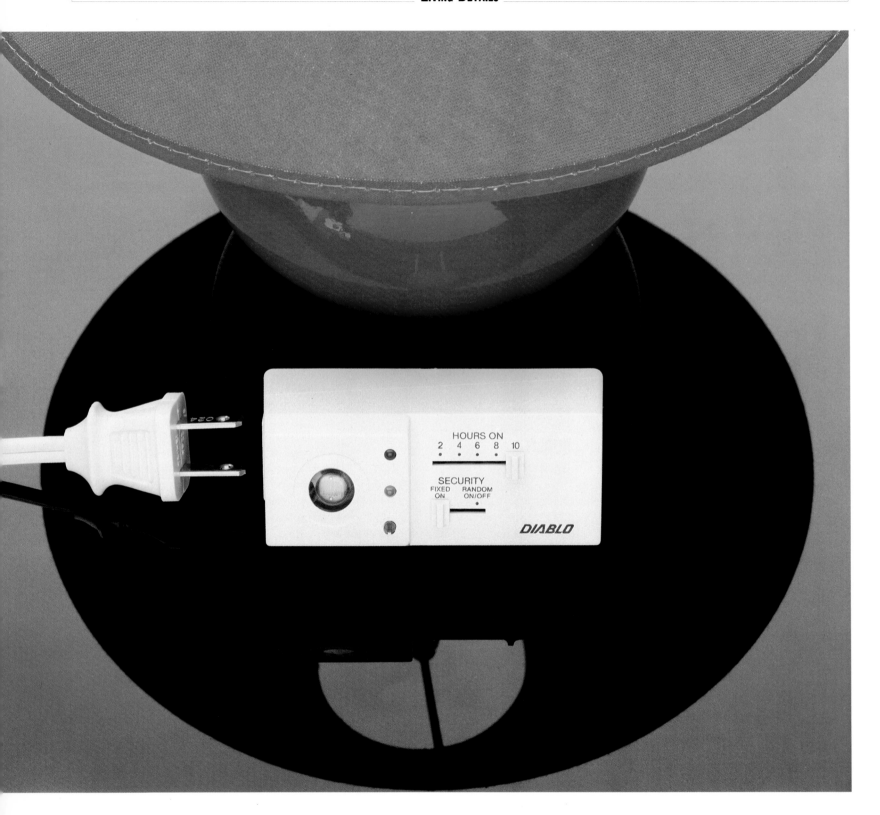

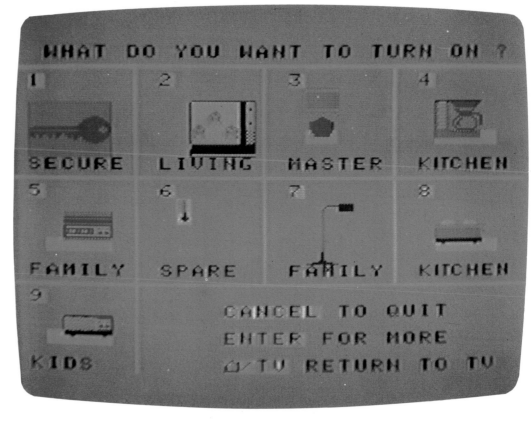

*A wave from the future, HomeMinder from GE is a complete remote control center for lights, security, heat, air-conditioning, and much more (above, top, right). This ingenious stash lets you slip valuables between the pages (above, top, left). Hide an extra key outside in this hollow rock (above, bottom). A dark house always draws attention, so let this timer turn on the lights even if you aren't home (left).*

ple wires that run along baseboards. Smoke detectors can be connected to this system, and some models have remote "panic transmitters" that can be carried from room to room and pushed to sound the alarm if you hear suspicious sounds outside the house.

Motion detectors are wonderful alarm devices for apartments because they require no installation. These self-contained units sit on a table or shelf, emitting either high-frequency ultrasonic waves or radio waves, depending on whether it is an ultrasonic or microwave model. The waves cover an area of 500 square feet or more, creating an entrapment area of invisible waves. Any intrusion into the area breaks the wave pattern that is bouncing back to the alarm unit, and triggers the alarm.

Microwaves are more versatile than ultrasonic waves and can be aimed at specific areas, such as a hallway or a wall containing windows. Both types of motion detector, however, suffer from false alarms caused by unpreventable movement, such as curtains blowing in the wind, pets wandering through the room, or windows vibrating. However, the better models have sensitive adjustments that may help to eliminate many of these false alarms.

Whatever your living situation, run a security check all around your home. Inspect windows and doors with the eye of a thief, and if you find any vulnerable entry points, consider changing your security system so it will delay and discourage thieves, if not prevent them from breaking in altogether.

# A COMFORTABLE CLIMATE

W hat can you do about noisy neighbors, an apartment that is too cold in winter and too hot in summer, inadequate ventilation, or the invasion of roaches and other unwanted pests? Each of these problems can make even a terrific apartment or first home an uncomfortable place to live. Solving these problems is often not as easy as painting a wall or buying a new area rug for the living room. Nevertheless, these conditions are not hopeless. There are some reasonable improvements that you can initiate to make life more livable. None requires major restructuring of the premises, and those that are a bit expensive can be taken with you when you move.

## COOLING YOUR HOME IN SUMMER

When buying air-conditioners, there are many factors to keep in mind and no pat answers.

First, consider air quality control. Many apartments built today are air-conditioned, but if you live in an older building that doesn't have centralized air-conditioning, invest in a window unit that can go with you when you move. In the event that your next home has air-conditioning, you can always sell your unit, perhaps even to the next tenant or through an ad in the newspaper. You might even consider a second-hand air-conditioner yourself if you

think you might only use it for one summer. Check it out thoroughly, however, before you buy it, listening carefully for rattles, buzzes, clicks, and other irritating noises.

Today's air-conditioners are available in a wide variety of sizes and powers. Check with a dealer before buying. Know the square-footage of the room you intend to cool so that the model you buy is powerful enough to be effective. On the other hand, don't grab the high-powered turbo model if you don't really need it. Consider which rooms need to be cooled and take along a floor plan to show the dealer. Cold air doesn't turn corners well, so you may have to settle for air-conditioning only one or two rooms in your house or just the front or the back of your apartment. An air-conditioner will work overtime if it is located in direct sunlight. Placed on a shady side of the building, a unit will be more effective with less strain.

Base your consideration of which rooms need cooling on which you use at various times of the day or night. If you are at work during the day and don't need the entire apartment or house cooled in the evening, a small one-room model in the bedroom may suffice. Also consider how long it will take to cool the area if you turn the air-conditioner off during working hours when you're not home. You'll save money on utility bills this way, but you may not want to wait for a large area to cool off when you come home.

An air-conditioner can often present decorating problems. Some apartments, for example, have small units built into the walls at inconvenient locations, such as three feet from the floor in the middle of a wall. How can you arrange your room so airflow is not blocked in summer, and how can you

Besides cooling the air, a ceiling fan can lend beauty and style to a room. Here, the wooden fan blades complement the wooden posts and beams and their rotating motion harmonizes well with the swirling pattern of the table stand (facing page). Large rooms, especially if they are used for cooking, cry out for proper air circulation. The vintage ceiling fan in this loft room seems right at home with other objects—such as the grandfather clock and the old-fashioned sign boards—that evoke a more leisurely past (left). This variation of the ceiling fan is ideal for a high-tech decorative scheme. It runs on a track, so it can be moved wherever the need is greatest. In cooler seasons, the fan unit itself can be easily replaced by a track light (above).

hide the eyesore that most air-conditioners become in winter? One technique is to build bookshelves on the wall around the unit. When the air-conditioner is not in use, place books in front to hide it. In summer, remove the books so air can come through.

In some climates, air-conditioners are not really necessary, since a window fan works just as well. The advantage of a window fan is that it can be removed when the hot season is over so you have full use of the window. A model with both intake and exhaust settings is quite useful. To cool the entire apartment, close all the other windows on the side where the fan is located, open the windows on the opposite side, and set the fan for "out" or exhaust. The fan will pull in cooler air through the open windows while eliminating stale odors. Often at night if all the windows in the apartment are closed except those in the bedroom, a window fan set on exhaust will create a wonderful breeze across the bed.

On a really hot day if you want to use the room with the fan in it, turn it on "intake." Often a low speed will create enough air circulation to keep the room pleasant. Moving air always makes a room feel cooler.

Once you become accustomed to a fan, you may never again want the chilly, ice-box feeling of an air-conditioner. Many people who prefer fans find that because their bodies have to adjust less to the outside temperature in summer, they aren't bothered by the heat as badly as when they spend most of the day in air-conditioned buildings, then have to adjust to the extreme change when they go outside.

Another easy, but often overlooked cooling device is a ceiling fan. The quiet, gentle circulation that it creates can make a room comfortable on the hottest of days, and the fan uses much less electricity than an air-conditioner. Relatively inexpensive, ceiling fans are not much more difficult to install than an overhead light fixture, and they can be taken with you when you move. The fan can be installed in the same electrical fixture as a ceiling light. To do this, turn off the power, remove the light, and replace it with a fan, using the same wiring, but be sure to follow the installation directions. If the fan has several speeds, you'll have to replace the switch that controls the fixture with one that has multiple positions.

If there is no overhead light in the room, a ceiling fan can be installed on the surface of the ceiling. Follow the manufacturer's instructions, and be sure to screw the fan to a ceiling joist. Run wires across the ceiling to a junction box, according to building code standards. Conceal the cord in a metal casing painted the same color as the ceiling or, if the room has a beamed ceiling, run the cord along a beam. Another alternative is to use the ceiling model that has a swag cord that can be looped across the ceiling and run down the wall to an electrical outlet.

## HEATING PROBLEMS IN WINTER

To solve the problem of retaining heat in the winter, various types of weather stripping and plastic film have been developed that are quite effective. Weather stripping applied around the windows and frames will seal the gaps there and keep a lot of heat inside.

Polyethylene film stretched across a window and, when sealed tightly around the casement, will also retain

*A cast-iron wood-burning stove is an efficient supplementary heat source during the cold winter months (facing page, top). A translucent weather screen mounted over shutters prevents heat from escaping through a large window, while offering a gentle, luminous glow during the day and consolidating to resemble a light-colored wall at night (facing page, bottom). In a room this size, with high ceilings and lots of nooks and crannies, a freestanding wood-burning stove is an attractive, cost-effective heater (above).*

heat. The problem is that they also cut down somewhat on sunlight and create a milky cast to the view out the window. They also inhibit ventilation; some windows will have to be opened periodically to let stale air out and fresh air in. Plastic film works well, however, if you live in a large rambling apartment or house and can close off some rooms or windows during the coldest months. You can cut down on heating costs, too, if you leave some rooms unheated, seal the windows, close the door when the room is not in use, and let warm air from the rest of the house heat the room when it is in use.

Another heat retention method is an insulation mat that is fitted into the window at night or during the day when you aren't home. Since a great deal of heat escapes through the glass in window panes (even in well-constructed windows), covering them with insulation board will allow less heat to escape through the surface of the glass. You can turn the heat down low at night and still be warm or keep the temperature relatively stable though the thermostat is set on low when you are not at home. You can make your own insulation mat out of rigid foam that is cut to fit snuggly into the window and wrapped with polyethylene to create a vapor barrier. Cover the mat with a decorative fabric, and sew tabs made of the fabric to the edges for easy removal. At night simply push the board into place and remove it in the morning.

Another possibility is an insulated shade. You can either buy shades with magnetic tape along the edge and the bottom that seals it tightly along the window frame, or you can make your own out of quilted material lined with insulated vapor barrier. Sew velcro or apply magnetic tape to the edges of the shades and along the casement.

## SOUND-PROOFING TECHNIQUES

No home is completely soundproof; there are only degrees of sound-resistance. Drapes along a wall will muffle noise that passes through it— from either direction, by the way, in case you like your music loud and late. A carpet on the floor will help to muffle your own noise and make things quieter for the people beneath you, as will raising speakers up off the floor. Stretched fabric on a wall, or across a frame that hangs on a wall, has the acoustical effect of deadening sound by eliminating hard wall surfaces where sound reverberates.

If you live on a noisy street, consult local dealers of shades and blinds about the newest acoustical materials and designs. Some blinds have acoustical properties that muffle the noise coming through while still allowing light and air to enter. Heavy drapes at a window will also keep some noise out.

## AIR QUALITY

If the quality of the air in your home is less than desirable, you might need a humidifer or a dehumidifer, especially for comfortable sleeping. In extremely dry climates, a humidifier will increase the amount of moisture in the air. In wet, humid climates, a dehumidifier will remove moisture. Both devices bring the level of moisture in the air into the range where it is easiest to breathe. Ionizers alter the ion balance

A bathroom with a large window can be very uncomfortable when a cold wind is blowing. A heater will make the room warm, but it won't block the breeze. The solution is an insulated shade that matches the wall and the shower curtain and can be lowered when needed (left). Hot air and fumes rise, so an air conditioner installed on a wall near the ceiling with controls below makes good sense. This placement also leaves valuable window and working space undisturbed. A range hood helps to remove smoke and odors quickly (right).

in the atmosphere by changing positively charged ions to negatively charged ones. Some people believe that these negative ions bond with positive ones to make them feel good, but on a more concrete level, ionizers help to eliminate static cling. And simply using the exhaust setting on the window fan will eliminate stale or musty odors.

Odors from nearby factories, alleys, or sewage disposals can be a real nuisance. Since you can't keep the windows permanently closed, the best tactic is to try to cover the offending odors by adding alternative scents to your home. Sachets, candles, incense, or eucalyptus boughs will help. Another trick is to put drops of potpourri oil on light bulbs. As the oil heats, it releases a fresh-smelling scent.

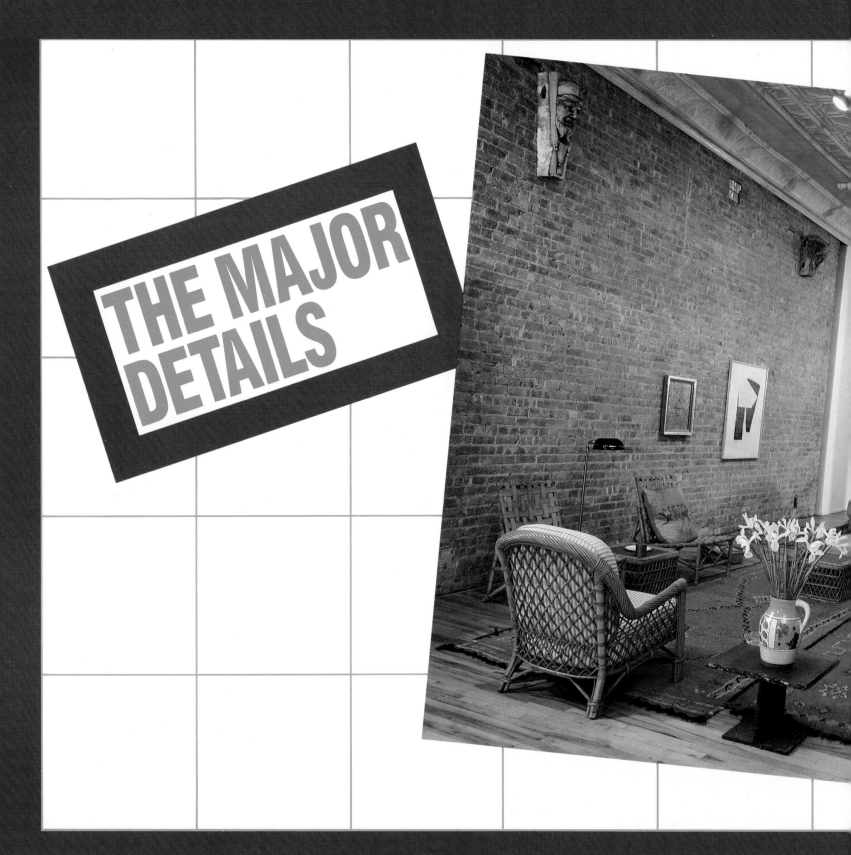

# THE MAJOR DETAILS

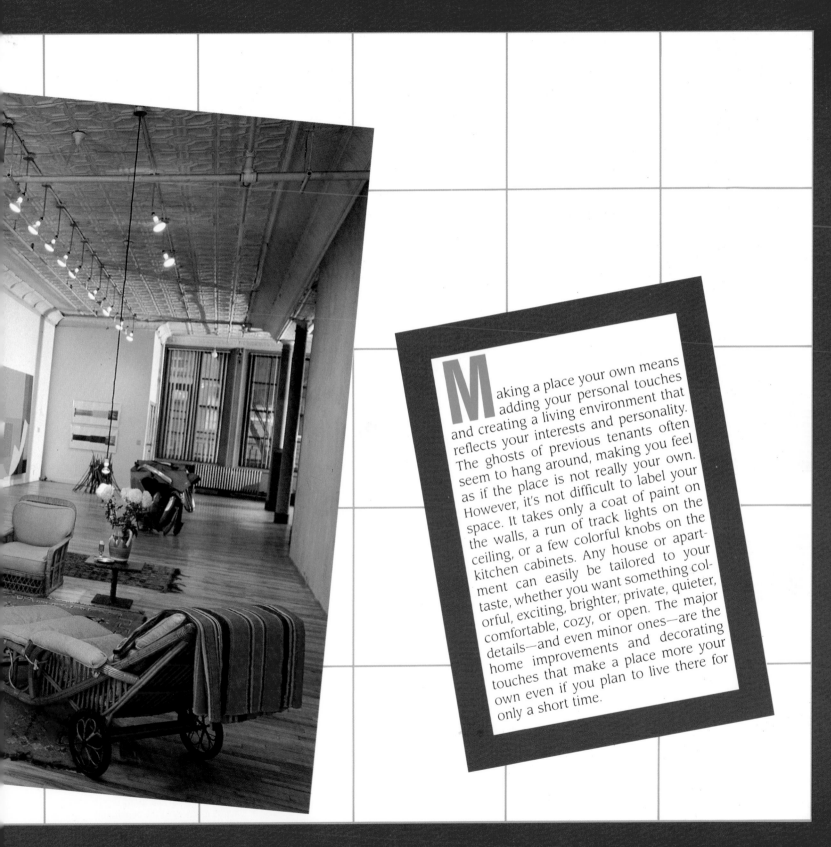

Making a place your own means adding your personal touches and creating a living environment that reflects your interests and personality. The ghosts of previous tenants often seem to hang around, making you feel as if the place is not really your own. However, it's not difficult to label your space. It takes only a coat of paint on the walls, a run of track lights on the ceiling, or a few colorful knobs on the kitchen cabinets. Any house or apartment can easily be tailored to your taste, whether you want something colorful, exciting, brighter, private, quieter, comfortable, cozy, or open. The major details—and even minor ones—are the home improvements and decorating touches that make a place more your own even if you plan to live there for only a short time.

# WALLS, FLOORS, AND CEILINGS

*Flowers perched on a stand near the ceiling add an unexpected dash of romance (left). Colorful trim calls attention to exquisite period ceiling molding (above). A whimsical stencil pattern adds an interesting border and a sense of loftiness to this cheerful room (right).*

Before you begin to organize and decorate a room, look around at the basics—walls, ceilings, and floors. Are the floors dull and dirty? Is the paint on the walls chipped or cracked? Are the ceilings stained? No matter how well you decorate a room, you can't possibly conceal unattractive smudges and spots or an old, faded paint job. Furniture and decorative items can be moved around and re-placed, but the walls, ceilings, and floors of a room remain. A wise home-improver will tackle these basic sur-faces before going on to the furniture and decorative touches.

## REPAIRING WALLS AND CEILINGS

Wallboard can be dented or broken rather easily, but luckily it's not difficult to repair. Simply draw a rectangle around the damaged area, making sure the corners are true right angles. Drill three-quarter-inch starter holes inside the rectangle and then cut out the rec-tangle with a keyhole saw. Cut two pieces of one-by-three-inch wood boards, each about six inches longer than the rectangle's vertical side. At-tach each piece behind the wall with wallboard screws so that about half of the piece is showing through the open-ing. Then cut a patch of wallboard the size of the opening and attach it with wallboard screws to the braces. Spread a thin layer of joint compound over the seams and then tape them, smoothing the tape down and embedding it with a putty knife. Allow the joint compound to dry for twenty-four hours. Sand any rough spots down and then apply at least three more coats of compound over the seams, allowing each to dry thoroughly before adding the next one.

To seal a hairline crack, first widen it slightly with a pointed can opener so you can insert a substantial amount of joint compound. Clear out dust and loose debris. Fill the crack with joint compound so that it spreads over onto the good wall surface. Allow it to dry for a day; if the patch subsides, fill it to the surface again. Let it dry and then sand it smooth.

If you have a large hole in a plaster wall, chip and knock away all the loose plaster around the hole. This may enlarge the hole a bit, but that's not difficult to repair. Undercut the plaster

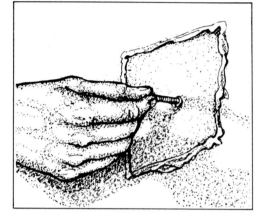

*To repair a small hole in the wallboard, insert a small saw in the hole, then cut a square around the outside of the hole. Remove wallboard piece. Cut a patch the same size and shape as the square piece you just removed. Insert a screw in the middle of the patch to act as a handle, then apply joint compound all around the edges. Put the patch in position, holding it in place by the screw (above, top). Let the joint compound dry for a day, then remove the screw. Spread compound over the whole patch with a trowel (above, bottom), and let dry for a day again. Sand the compound, then paint the patch the same color as the rest of the wall.*

To fill a small hole or a hairline crack in a plaster wall, begin by knocking away any loose plaster with a can opener (below). Clear out dust and loose debris. Fill the crack or hole with joint compound, letting it spread onto the intact wall surface (right). Allow it to dry for a day. If the compound subsides, fill it, then let it dry again. Sand the surface smooth.

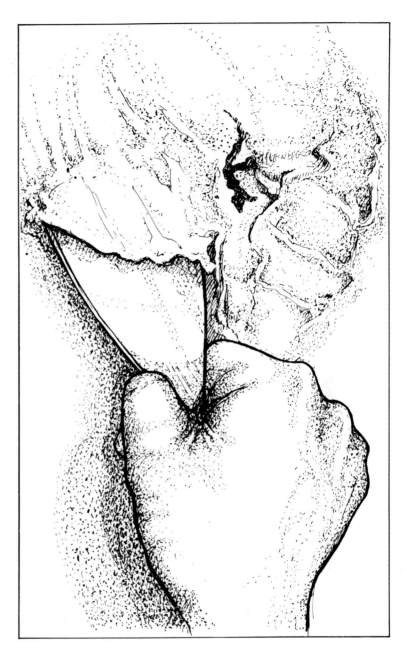

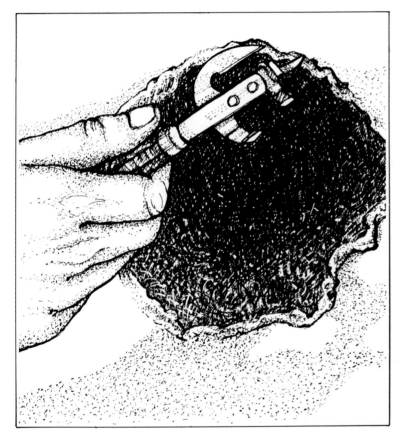

around the edge of the hole with a can opener, digging out the plaster so that it slopes from the edge toward the wooden lattice work, called the lath, that is behind the plaster. Wet the edge of the hole with water and fill it with plaster, covering the lath evenly. Stop when the new plaster is just below the level of the surrounding wall. Score the plaster with a putty knife so the next coat will adhere firmly. Allow the plaster to dry and then apply joint compound over it, feathering the edges into the surrounding surface. Let it dry overnight, then sand it smooth.

For a small hole in a plaster ceiling, soak newspaper in plaster, crumple it up, and stuff it in the hole, pushing it between the strips of lath. Fill the hole with plaster to about one-quarter inch below the surface, and let it dry. Then wet the patch and add one more coat of finish plaster. Smooth the edges with a straightedge.

## A NEW PAINT JOB

The simplest way to dress up any room is to give it a good paint job. It's not expensive if you shop around for paint sales at hardware or department stores. A few gallons of paint will be well worth the money. Even if you only stay in your place a year, or the paint job is just a stopgap until you can afford to do more extensive redecorating, you'll immediately appreciate the personalized feel of the room.

*The artist's touch shows in this exuberant paint job that works surprisingly well in this Memphis-inspired foyer. The assymetrical angles of the doorway, flagstones, and carpeting are tied together with fun and flair by the patchwork of colors on the wall and ceiling (facing page, left). Here is a truly enchanting room where usual boundaries disappear and the commonplace is rendered magical. The color of the walls seeps into the ceiling and a pair of painted banners cross overhead creating a false corner (facing page, right). A sophisticated, tailored look is achieved by means of a subtly textured cloth wall covering that blends with floor-length drapes and wall-to-wall carpeting (right).*

There are two basic types of interior paint—latex and alkyd. Latex is a water-based paint that is odorless, quick drying, and easily cleaned up with water. Alkyd paint is more expensive, but it adheres better to surfaces and offers a more durable and richer-looking finish. If you use alkyd paint, you'll also have to use paint thinner and cleaning solvents. Be sure to keep the room you are painting well ventilated to allow for the paint's slow drying time.

If you use a latex paint, only use brushes with synthetic bristles. Natural bristles absorb water from latex and become clogged. They'll clump up and make painting difficult. To judge the quality of a brush before buying it, grab the bristles and see if they feel full and thick. Press the bristles against a hard surface and watch to see if they fan out smoothly. When released, they should quickly spring back together. Also try tugging on the bristles to see if they come out. If some do, the brush is not well made. As for size, match it to the job. A three-quarter-inch brush will handle large surfaces, such as the walls themselves, but you should also have a two-inch to two-and-a-half inch brush for narrower areas such as window sashes. You'll need a small one-inch to one-and-a-half-inch brush for the trim.

In addition to brushes, buy a couple of rollers. The frames and covers for rollers are in standard sizes. Covers come in short, medium, and long nap. Most interior walls look best when paint is applied with a medium-nap roller, because it leaves a faint stipple on the surface. If the walls are very uneven or porous, a long-nap roller will hold more paint and work it into the indentations in the surface. Other equipment for a standard paint job includes a stirrer, drop cloth, roller pan, ladder, rags, and paint cleaner.

The success of any paint job depends on the surface that is being painted. Paint can only adhere properly to a surface that is free of dust, grease, and dirt and that is completely dry. Never paint over chipped or cracked paint. A new paint job will not fill cracks or "glue" the flaking paint back to the wall, but will merely adhere to the surface on which it is put. If you paint over a peeling surface, the paint will peel right off. Similarly, old cracks will return through the new paint. You can paint or paper over wallpaper if there is only one layer of it and it isn't bubbling or peeling. However, wallpaper can be easily removed with a wallpaper steamer (that can be rented) or with chemical solvents.

To get a room ready to be painted, remove most of the furniture and wall hangings. Cover any furniture that must remain in the room. Remove switch and outlet faces and all doorknobs. Cover light fixtures with plastic if they cannot be taken down. Clean the walls, remove badly chipped paint with a scraper, and patch any holes or cracks. Spread a good drop cloth over the floor. Also apply masking tape over the trim, baseboards, moldings, and along the outside edges of glass panes on the windows. If you are painting the entire room, begin with the ceiling, then do the walls and then the trim. Paint the doors and windows last.

Even though many paints are advertised as "one coat only," most paint jobs require two coats, especially if you are covering another color. Be patient and accept the fact that you will need to apply another coat. If you try to skimp by applying one coat too heavily, you won't get as good a finish as you will by applying one coat modestly, letting it dry, and adding a second coat.

*The walls and ceiling in this uncluttered bedroom do everything but turn you over and tuck you in. Sky surrounds the sleeper inside, then a fanciful skywriter's work carries him or her outside (left). A carefully planned wall treatment can overcome a room's awkward dimensions. This attic bedroom is small and has an irregularly sloped ceiling. To make its proportions even out, moldings are attached part of the way up each wall and horizontal to the floor. This line detracts from the slope in the ceiling. To enhance the effect, the walls are painted a solid white below the molding and papered above in wallpaper with a delicate, peaceful design that complements the country furnishings. The vertical lines in the design create the impression that the walls are taller than they actually are (right).*

## WALLPAPER

Wallpaper is another option for sprucing up a room. Many people who rent believe that wallpaper is a costly improvement for walls that belong to someone else. By and large, that's true. While paint can be bought on sale, often for about ten dollars a gallon, wallpaper can be very expensive. Nevertheless, wallpaper can sometimes be found on sale. If you buy just a few rolls to add accent to a room or to paper a small alcove or even one wall, the effect can turn an otherwise average room into one with more character.

Today, when most wallcoverings come in pretrimmed and prepasted rolls, it is not a difficult task to paper. Wallcoverings are packaged in thirty-six-square-foot rolls, though only about thirty feet of each roll will be used by the time each strip is cut and fit properly. To estimate the number of rolls you will need, measure the perimeter of the area, then multiply that measurement by the height of the area. Divide the total by thirty square feet for the number of rolls needed.

Prepare the walls for papering in the same way you would to paint, though you do not need to tape around the moldings and outlets. To make sure your paper hangs squarely on the wall, drop a string with a weight at the bottom from the ceiling about ten inches from the corner or starting edge of the wall. Chalk a line along the string. You will use this mark to align your first strip of wallcovering. Then align all subsequent strips with the previous strip. Be sure to establish a new chalk line as you start each wall.

To actually hang the paper, cut a strip slightly longer—about three inches—than the height of the wall. If the paper is prepasted, immerse the strip in a wallpaper tray, which is probably sold at the wallcovering store, or in a tub. It usually helps to roll the strip up before you immerse it, then unroll it so it becomes completely wet. If you are not using prepasted paper, lay the strip on a table or on the floor and spread wallpaper adhesive over it with a paste brush. Lay the strip on the wall from the top down, being careful to align it with the chalk line or the previous strip. Smooth the whole piece with a wide wallpaper brush to remove any air bubbles. Finally, with a razor blade, trim the extra paper from the bottom of the strip along the molding, and around the electrical outlets or the windows.

## CORK TILES

Cork tiles make an attractive, practically maintenance-free wallcovering, especially in an odd nook where you want a different texture to contrast with the rest of the room. They're good sound insulators for television and stereo rooms, and near phones, desks, or hobby areas, cork tiles serve as large bulletin boards. Some tiles come with adhesive backing and are easy to install. With others, you'll have to put a coat of adhesive on the wall first.

To determine the number of tiles you need to buy, measure the length of the wall you intend to cover and mark the midpoint near the floor as a reference point. Lay a run of tiles on the floor and check the tile that crosses the midpoint. If less than half the tile is on the left side, measure half a tile-width to the left of the midpoint and use that as the midpoint. If less than half is on the right side, measure to the right. Using a carpenter's level or a plumb line, mark a vertical guideline down the wall. Then measure down from the ceiling for as many tile-widths as needed to reach eye level. Mark that point as a horizontal guideline. Be sure the guidelines

cross at right angles so the tiles will align properly. Then begin by attaching the first tile in one quadrant at the cross point. Lay a few more in that quadrant and then do the same in the other three, fanning out in all four directions to cover the entire wall. Leave a slight space between them for expansion. Cork tiles can be cut to fit the borders. If a tile breaks or crumbles while you are working with it, simply reunite the pieces and glue them on the wall. Finish the job by pressing the tiles into the adhesive with a rolling pin, moving it diagonally across several tiles at a time. Stubborn tiles can be fastened with a finishing nail.

*Cover a whole wall in cork tile or just a part of it. Finish the edges of the section with pieces of light-colored moulding, and you'll have a great place to display photographs—old and new—or any other collection that will make an intriguing wall covering (above).*

*Wallpaper design can be repeated successfully in other furnishings to give the entire room a coordinated look. Grey-striped wallpaper is mimicked by a grey-striped apron, stacked white dishes, and a grey, black, and white print (facing page, left). A floral print in the wallpaper is picked up in a layer of window drapery, but tempered by a color-coordinated watered silk design (left).*

71

A thick wooden trim offers a snug recess for a wall of mirror sections, adding depth to a long, narrow living and dining room (facing page). Set flush against a sloping wall, the upper mirror reflects sunlight, a window view, and vertical lines from the opposite wall. The lower mirror extends the pattern of the tile floor, creating a mocking contrast (left). A curtained bed with a headboard mirror looks twice as romantic and inviting (right).

## MIRROR TILES

Mirror tiles can transform a room, creating the illusion that it is larger than it really is. Mounted on an interior wall, they will reflect daylight from windows across from them, thus providing sources of natural light deep inside the room. Take care to install them evenly so that the reflections are not distorted.

Mirror tiles must be firmly attached to the wall so they won't shift or fall off. They are mounted like cork tiles. First,

lay out the guidelines in the same manner. Be sure to attach the tile to a clean, dry wall starting from the marked midpoint. If they don't have adhesive backing, use double-sided tape; just peel the protective backing off one side of the tape and stick a square of it near each corner of the tile, then remove the rest of the backing and press the tile to the wall. Lightweight tiles can be cut at home to fit at the border. First mark where the cut is to be on the mirror's surface, then score it with a glass cutter, using a straightedge to assure a straight line. Finally, hold the tile firmly on a table and snap it along the cut.

## HANGING THINGS ON WALLS

No matter how the surface of the walls are treated, most people feel that a home does not reflect its owner until something has been hung on the walls. And there is no doubt that pictures, paintings and wallhangings are an easy way to label your territory.

There's no magic needed to hang things on a wall so that they stay put. The secret is to take into account two

Fabric draped in gentle folds covers an entire wall to define a formal dining area in this large, windowless room (facing page, right). Amid all the eyecatching metal furniture in this boy's room, a bicycle stored on the wall saves space and looks stunning (above). A glass-brick wall twists and turns light and reflections to effectively and artistically designate an entrance hall (right).

things: the type of wall, and the weight and size of the object.

There are two kinds of walls: hollow and solid. Hollow walls are usually wallboard or plaster mounted over wood studs located sixteen inches apart. Solid walls are made of concrete, brick, or plaster over some form of masonry.

To hang something on a hollow wall, you have several options. Locate the stud nearest the spot where you want to hang the object by measuring sixteen-inch sections from a corner or by using a magnetic stud-finder, which you can get at a hardware store. Then hang the object on a nail driven through the wall and into the stud, or on a nail-mounted fastener designed to support the weight of the object you want to hang.

If you want to hang something where there is no stud, buy a special toggle bolt or an expansion anchor at a hardware store. Both operate on the same principle. They are driven through the wall and expand to grip the wall from behind. The toggle bolt has "wings" that are held closed under spring tension. When the bolt is driven through the surface, the wings fly open. An expansion anchor is put into a hole that has been drilled to its diameter;

when screwed in tightly the body of the anchor expands behind the wall.

To hang something on a solid wall, the easiest method is to use masonry nails simply driven into the wall. A more complicated way, but one that will prevent the plaster or masonry from chipping and loosening the hanger, is to use a plug or wall anchor. Each is seated in a hole drilled into the wall and acts as a kind of sleeve for a screw that, in turn, jams the plug or anchor into the wall and holds the object you intend to hang.

For lightweight objects, such as mounted posters or small framed photos, an adhesive picture hook may be all that's needed. Be sure the wall surface behind the adhesive is clean and dry before applying the hook. A picture hook that is nailed into the wall, even through a hollow between studs, will be strong enough to hold up to twenty pounds. If you are unfamiliar with the great variety of wall fasteners available on the market, drop by a local hardware store before you hang your object and ask the clerk what is recommended for the job. There's sure to be a fastener that's just right for the job.

## FIXING FLOORS

Almost every home has a few floor boards that squeak. It doesn't necessarily mean there is anything structurally wrong with the floor, but the squeak can be annoying. If you have just bought your home, now may not be the time to fully correct any serious problem, but it's not difficult to at least silence the squeak. Apartment-dwellers, too, should not have to put up

*The steeply pitched white ceiling of an attic apartment is delightfully tempered by the addition of bright red crossbeams (facing page). The lighting plan for this dining room takes full advantage of a high ceiling. An ornate chandelier and a contemporary floor lamp continue the same provocative mixture of styles that is exhibited by the eclectic mix of chairs (above).*

*The bold geometric pattern of this area rug underscores a carefully planned setting for socializing in this room designed by Miles J. Lourie. It also draws together design elements in the wall-mounted parts collection, the expressionistic painting, and the upholstery of the chairs (facing page). Hand-tufted rugs or wall hangings will add rich color and zestful detail to monochromatic rooms (above, left, and below).*

with the aggravating sound for the few years they will be in the apartment.

The most common cause of squeaks is two or more warped or loose boards rubbing against each other. There are several easy ways to silence them. If you can work from beneath the floor in the basement, locate the problem boards by having someone walk on them while you watch from below. Then gently tap wooden shims, or wedges, between the beam and the floor boards to prevent them from moving. Wedge the shim in just enough to prevent the board from moving, not so much that you separate the boards from the beam.

Another method is to drive metal glazier points (used for setting window panes in frames) into the space between two squeaking boards. First cover the glazier points with graphite or another dry lubricant, then set them below the surface of the floor, using a putty knife and a hammer to drive them in between the boards.

If you live in an apartment or a house where you don't have access to the basement, you can drive eight-penny nails into the boards to hold them solidly against the subfloor. Try to place them over beams if possible, and always position two nails in a criss-cross pattern. To prevent splitting a hardwood floor, drill a hole first and then insert the nail. To finish, hammer the nail to below the surface and fill the hole with wood putty that matches the color of the floor.

Refinishing a hardwood floor or laying new tiles or linoleum is a costly and time-consuming task that you probably won't want to take on. Besides, the only remedy that may be needed for a disappointing floor—whether it's hardwood, tile, or linoleum—is a thorough cleaning and waxing. Get down on your knees and get the dirt out from the

Gray-green walls emphasize the cool whiteness of this tiled bathroom floor. Stencilled trim midway up each wall and along the ceiling picks up the tile pattern, giving the entire room a well-organized appearance (facing page). Vinyl floor covering in red-and-white check suggests a fresh, clean tablecloth and injects flair into a simple, all-white design scheme (right).

corners and the cracks. Wash a varnished wood floor with lukewarm water only, but use detergent and water on dingy tile and linoleum. To remove old wax, use very hot water. Use paste wax and a rented floor buffer to polish a hardwood floor, although liquid wax and a mop will work fine on linoleum.

Tiles are usually glazed, and therefore don't need waxing.

The time and care you take to repair and clean up walls, ceilings, and floors will reflect on the overall look of the room. The color schemes and decorating ideas that you'll get from the photographs in this chapter are only success-

ful to the extent that the basic framework of the room itself is sound, clean, and pleasing to the eye. So spend a day or two preparing and repairing any imperfections. The time and money you put into decorative projects will not be wasted, and will be much more effective.

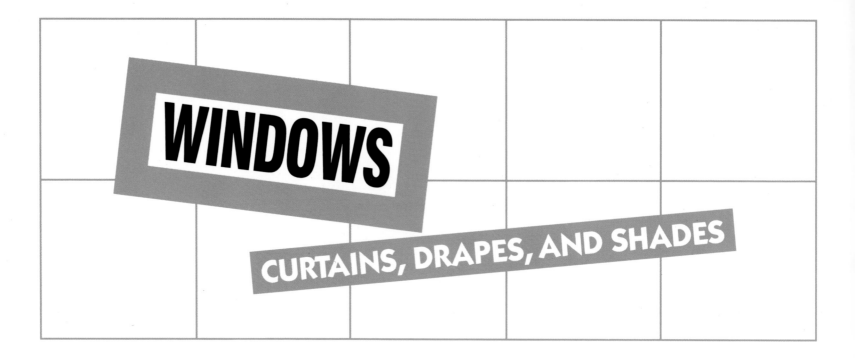

# WINDOWS

## CURTAINS, DRAPES, AND SHADES

The three great assets of windows—daylight, a view, and a sense of openness—are the very elements that are often eliminated by haphazard window treatments. Nevertheless, all three of these elements need some control, some manipulation. They are there to be emphasized or de-emphasized as the time and the mood determine. A window opened or closed, drapes drawn together or pulled back, blinds adjusted this way or that, a shade half drawn or down completely—these are the simple but effective ways we regulate the atmosphere of a room, depending on time of day or night, on whether we feel introspective or out-going, on whether we are engaged in a bright, open activity or one that requires shadow and privacy, whether we want the room to be open to the outdoors or sheltered against the cold or rain.

## MAKING THE BEST USE OF WINDOWS

Because windows are subject to frequent change and manipulation, it is important that their three greatest assets are not diminished by the way they are treated. In most rooms, windows are the primary source of natural light and may open onto a view that is rather common or one that is wonderfully breathtaking. Whatever decorating techniques you use on windows, take care to evaluate each window and its treatment specifically so that the results enhance the whole room and the activities planned for it.

In addition to controlling light and creating privacy, a window treatment can serve other functions, too. A window hung with the soft folds of curtains or drapes, for example, will break up the hard angular surfaces of a room, and temper its boxlike quality. The soft texture and the curved, flowing lines of fabric offer a necessary contrast in many rooms that would otherwise be hard, cold and stark.

The right treatment can also make a window appear larger than it actually is. Small uninteresting windows can be framed in drapes that reach from the floor to the ceiling and beyond the actual edge of the casement so that the overall effect, especially when the drapes are drawn, is that the window is much larger than it really is. And a line of two or three small windows can be given a single treatment so that they visually play the role of one larger window. Such an arrangement can give a wall whose windows break it up into

Bordered on the bottom by plants and on the sides by thin cascades of sheer fabric that spill onto the floor, this window truly functions as a gateway to the outdoors. Narrow-slatted white screens allow for the maximum amount of brightness, even when they are lowered completely (left). To preserve the purity and austerity of this bedroom, a bare minimum of window dressing is used: just enough to guarantee privacy and softened sunlight over the bed (top).

small segments a more solid and substantial look and a greater depth.

Pulling together a room's colors, motifs, or textures in the window treatment is a simple, effective way to unify an otherwise scattered room design. For instance, curtains that contain the major colors of the room will cause the eye to find consistency in the overall plan, even if you didn't have a unified plan to begin with.

The environmental features of windows should also be included in your decorating decisions. If a window faces north or toward the prevailing winds, you may want to treat it for the cold winter months. Heavy, insulated drapes, for example, will keep cold air out and help retain the room's heat. Conversely, a window with a southern exposure may need some means of filtering the hot sunlight in summer to keep the room cooler and prevent the sun from fading the rug or upholstery.

What are the options for window treatments? Traditional methods of covering windows include curtains, drapes, shades, blinds, shutters, and screens. In the right room, however, macrame, plants, and other ingenious tricks can provide the right amount of privacy and control light just as well.

A single drape of the same cloth used to upholster a nearby chair parts coyly to reveal a window. This arrangement conceals awkwardly truncated sections of the window casement and leaves space on the small wall for pictures (facing page). These generously proportioned and carefully detailed shutters add dramatic light and shadow effects to a room often filled with music. They also help to protect valuable furnishings from the damaging effects of direct sunlight (left). Suggesting a seraglio in eighteenth-century France, this imaginative window treatment filters light in a variety of seductive ways. It brings two enormous windows into an impressive scale more compatible with the furniture in the room (below).

# CURTAINS
# AND
# DRAPES

There are several styles and methods of hanging curtains. The most popular are two-way traverse curtains that consist of two straight-hanging panels that slide along a traverse rod and are operated by pull cords. Traverse curtains can also be "double hung" to give the window a layered look. The second or inside curtain is usually more sheer than the main curtain, allowing more light to enter the room. One-way traverse curtains function in a similar manner but consist of a single curtain that covers the entire window and is drawn back only to one side. Tie-back curtains usually run the width of the window and are tied back on each side, forming two graceful billows. Cafe curtains are short curtains mounted halfway up the window and consist of two panels hung from rings, which slip along a curtain rod. A second set may be installed at the top of the window for complete privacy. Combinations are also possible using cafe curtains with either tie-backs or traverse curtains. The possibilities are limited only by the type of window and your imagination.

Curtains can be hung either inside the window casings or outside them. If the casements themselves are attractive architectural features, you may want to leave them exposed, and hang curtains within them. If they are nothing special, extend the rod to the outer edges of the casement so that the curtains cover them.

Drapes are usually made of a heavier material than curtains and are hung either from the top of the window casement or from the ceiling line. Drapes

White drapes cover an entire wall of alternating windows and pillars in this loft apartment. Close them all, and you retain a bright, spacious atmosphere at night. Open them selectively, and you focus attention on specifically desired areas. Note the imaginative use of a window frame as a room divider (above). Beautiful floor-to-ceiling windows opening onto a yard beg for a dramatic window treatment. White muslin curtains are flung over high hooks during the day, and the result is a bit of instant theater. Objects that invoke nature are placed ceremoniously around the window to further strengthen this impression (facing page).

Full, billowing drapes mediate well between a huge, stark mirror and an oversized window whose casing resembles a Roman aqueduct. A matching valance restates the window's elliptical lines (above). An imaginative tie makes the curtain become more than just a window treatment; it is now a decorative accessory (right).

Lace cafe curtains and a lace valance suggest a kitchen in Paris. In this whimsical design, courtly cats watch over both indoors and outdoors (left). Rainbow curtains are the star attraction in this bedroom. They are left long and flowing to enhance their ephemeral feel (above).

extend to the floor and are thus more formal in appearance than curtains, which are contained closely around the window itself. A valance across the top gives drapes an even more imposing appearance. Using a drapery width wider than the actual window lets you cover more of the wall than just the window area. You can buy a rod of any width you want, depending on how much of the wall you want to cover with draperies. The rod does not have

to be limited by either the inside or outside measurement of the casement.

Measuring for drapes requires some tricky calculating. Be sure to add two inches for the overlap in the center and the necessary inches for the "returns" on each end of the rod, where the drape bends back toward the wall. Also allow additional material and space at each end of the rod (called "stack" space) where the drapes can be gathered when you expose the entire glass

area of the window. Calculate the stack area by dividing the glass width by three and adding twelve inches, then divide this figure by two. Mark this distance outside the casement from the outside edge of the glass on both sides. The distance between these two marks equals the length of the rod. The rod itself should be mounted at the ceiling line or four inches above the glass, so the hardware for the draperies cannot be seen from outside the house.

## SHADES AND BLINDS

Shades are one of the simplest ways of providing privacy and regulating light. The traditional, plain, off-white spring-roller shade is still a favorite, but designers have moved well beyond it in color and fabric. The shade cloth that for years has been a standard feature of windows now has such companion materials as fiberglass, vinyl, woven mesh, and other medium-weight fabrics. Color combinations and patterns

are almost limitless. Shades come in standard sizes, measured to the inside length and width of the casement.

There are different methods for operating shades. The spring-roller is the most common. When you release the tension, a spring mechanism pulls the shade up to the desired height. Roller shades, usually made of woven wood, are pulled up by two cords that loop around the shade and gradually draw it up into an ever larger roll. Roman shades pull the material up by panel sections that fold into a pleat behind each other. The bottom edge of a Roman shade is not as bulky as a roller shade. Austrian shades operate like Roman shades, but the bottom edge forms billowy scallops.

Most shades are lowered from top to bottom, but to allow light into the room, it's necessary to sacrifice some privacy at the bottom. An alternative design, good for urban dwellers whose neighbors' apartments often look directly into their own, is the bottom-to-top shades. Pulled part-way up, they still allow light to enter but offer privacy in the lower parts of the room. Bottom-to-top shades, as well as some top-to-bottom styles, have a valance across the top to hide the installation hooks and give them a more finished look.

If you want shades that hang inside the casement, first measure the casement's inside width in several places, since many windows are not true to square. Take the narrowest width and subtract half an inch for clearance. If you want shades that will be mounted outside the casement, measure the window casing from outer edge to outer edge. Trim wooden or bamboo shades with a fine-tooth saw. A shade with vinyl slats can be cut to fit with scissors. Always cut an equal amount from each side of the shade, and mark all the way down before you cut.

*Deep blue, semi-translucent window shades played against fire-engine red casements provide visual excitement in a child's room (facing page, left). Thin-slatted venetian blinds subdue harsh sunlight in this contemporary living room of muted tones (far left). Trailing ribbons accentuate the height of this tall, narrow window, adding loftiness to the room (left). A bamboo window blind contributes woodsy tones and textures to a predominantly black-and-white color scheme (above).*

Traditional venetian blinds now come in various styles, with slats as narrow as one-half-inch wide for a trim, sleek, high-tech look. A variety of colors are also available. For custom blinds, you can select colors and arrange them on the cords to create your own color spectrum.

Woven wooden blinds have an earthy, rugged look and are perfect for people who don't want the fussy, formal appearance of fabric window treatments. Nevertheless, there are a number of options within this category, depending on whether you want wood or yarn to predominate in the blind. Some blinds are mostly wood, others mostly yarn. The color of the yarn will also determine how brightly the blind stands out in the room or blends in with more neutral colors. Even the wooden slats can be painted bright colors if you want to avoid wood tones.

One of the greatest innovations for city apartment dwellers in recent years is the adaptation of vertical blinds for domestic use. Formerly found only in such commercial settings as offices, stores, and lobbies, vertical blinds are now being used in living quarters. The advantage of vertical blinds is that they offer greater privacy from neighbors whose apartments often look into each other from odd angles. The slats rotate a complete 180 degrees, so they can effectively block a view from any direction while at the same time allowing light to enter the room. Some types open from side to side, others from the center to both sides. The louvers come in varying degrees of translucence, from solid metal that will block all light to a thin vinyl that bathes the window area in a bright, milky light even when the blinds are closed. One final—but very important—advantage is that vertical blinds are much easier to clean than traditional venetian blinds.

*In this unusually proportioned children's room, wall and window treatments cooperate to provide a sense of balance and harmony (above). Thick-slatted vertical blinds have the linear design of draperies and the functional appeal of shutters. Vertical blinds spanning an entire wall produce any number of subtle lighting effects to grace this serene, Japanese-inspired bedroom (facing page).*

## SHUTTERS AND SCREENS

Two other options are available for people who want to avoid fabric at their windows—shutters and screens. The simple, wooden louvered shutters are handsome in their natural state, or they can be stained or painted to blend with other wood grains or colors in the room. Style options include adjustable louvers, nonadjustable louvers, and solid panels that can be painted or covered with fabric or wallpaper.

Unfinished shutters are available at hardware and lumber stores in single panels of varying widths. Measure your window and decide how wide the panels should be and how many of them you need. Panels are fastened together with hinges. When you measure your windows, decide whether you want shutters on both sides that meet in the middle, or one shutter that folds out from one side and reaches across to the other. The one-shutter arrangement folds up, accordian fashion, so lay out the panels before you mount them to be sure the hinges are fastened so that the panels fold up properly.

Shoji screens are translucent panels that create a bright, milky illumination at the window. Mounted in tracks, they slide back and forth to open and close.

Their spare Oriental design fits in well with the plain surfaces and clean angularity of minimalist decorating.

## LOW-COST WINDOW TREATMENTS

When living in a rented dwelling or a home that you have recently purchased, you won't want to invest heavily in window treatments that may be the wrong size or style for your next home or for the decor you choose

A flush of warm and woody light coming through white-painted shutters forms the perfect background for this contemporary pine sofa (left). Shoji panels mounted in front of the window on sliding tracks create a refined atmosphere (below). A noble window on the landing is appropriately dressed with two rows of richly hued wooden shutters. Their dark color creates a sense of depth in this narrow space (right).

when you have the time and money to decorate completely. Here are some tricks and ideas for economizing in window treatments.

Drapes do not have to close over the entire window if you are not concerned about regulating light or ensuring privacy. Slim panels that remain stationary on each side of the window require less material and are, therefore, appreciably less expensive than full drapes. They can be tied back if you want to avoid a severe vertical look.

Bed sheets can be used to create inexpensive window treatments. They must be cut and sewn carefully, so the patterns or designs match properly. Hang them from traverse rods or attach wooden rings along the top edge to hang on a cafe curtain rod. An even easier method is to just run an expandable extension rod through the top overlap of the sheet.

Often a window will look sufficiently trimmed with just a simple valance across the top made from attractive fabric. The window can then be finished with a shade or shutters if privacy is a concern. Another option is to build a cornice to trim the top of a window. Decide on the width of the cornice—perhaps five or six inches. Select a board five or six inches wide, depending on how wide you want the cornice to be. Then, cut the board to the width of the window, measured from the outside edges of the casement. Last, cut two end pieces from the board, each five inches long. Screw the three pieces together at right angles. Paint the finished cornice to match or contrast with the walls, or cover it with fabric stapled tightly in place. Mount the cornice on the window casement with wood screws, or use angle irons to mount it to the wall. The window can then be fitted with a shade to control light and privacy.

*Plastic window blinds are durable, easy to mount and maintain, and mix well with any style of furnishings. In this large upstairs room, neatly tailored plastic blinds with matchstick slats permit a maximum amount of light (left). Artist Charles Guilioli creates a window into paradise by painting on wooden shades. He uses only pastel colors so as not to overwhelm the room (above).*

Another decorating trick is to create a macrame design that will cover the window. Although there is a fine art to creating intricate macrame, a simple arrangement can be constructed with hemp and three dowels. Fasten as many strands of hemp as you need for privacy to three dowels, one at the top, one at the bottom, and one in the middle of the window. Tie the strands together, stringing in beads, driftwood, or other small objects so that the result is a design either tightly or loosely constructed to provide the amount of privacy you need.

To cover windows cheaply but with a personal touch, weave strands of colored yarn or ribbon into an inexpensive bamboo shade. Wind strands over and under the warp threads on the shade to create as wide a belt of color as you want. Vary the colors and the widths of their bands to create your own striped pattern. The result is a lively bamboo shade with a custom-made look.

You can also easily and inexpensively make a new shade from an old roller shade whose paper cloth is worn or stained. Simply remove the old paper and replace it with a medium-weight fabric, cut long enough to wrap around the wooden roller and wide enough at the sides to fold a hem. Machine-stitch the hems, then staple the fabric so it completely covers the roller.

Windows can present a challenge if your budget is limited at this time or you are making an investment in a temporary home. While traditional window treatments are always appropriate, they can be rather costly. Let your imagination go beyond the traditional, however, in deciding how extensively you need to control light and privacy, and then experiment with materials and creative arrangements that fit your budget and make sense for the length of time you plan to live with them.

# LIGHTING

Some rooms feel good to be in; others elicit an uneasy, disconcerted feeling. Lighting is often the crucial determinant, creating mood, drawing the separate elements of a room together, or highlighting individual features in their own right. A clever lighting pattern can hide a room's flaws, emphasize its strong points, enhance the color combinations, and draw the eye to what you want the visitor to see and notice. Investing in the right lamps and lighting fixtures is an inexpensive way to change the character of a room and let it express your personality.

Light is a creative power that can bring a room to life. It can manipulate space, creating the illusion of more space or smaller space. It can define a space for certain activities or occasions. It can screen out areas, either by putting them into shadow or by draw-

*Light fixtures that resemble sconces are beautiful and save space when attached to the wall (above). A stylized flying saucer hovers over a table and casts just the right amount of light (facing page).*

ing attention away from them. If you're giving a dinner party, for example, and you don't have separate living and dining rooms, you can focus attention on the living area early in the evening, when guests will be there, by dimming the lights over the dinner table. When dinner is served, you can brighten the lights over the table and dim the ones in the living area. Track lights running between the living and dining areas can be aimed at the respective spaces or pinpointed directly downward to create a curtain of light beams that visually and artistically separate the two halves of the room.

What should be illuminated? Not just "the room." A room is made up of many parts, some of which you may not have considered worthy of their own light source. Tables and chairs are almost always lit, but consider the walls, ceilings, floor, passageways, and hallways. Lighting should enhance the interesting architectural features of a room. Use light, for instance, to set off a brick wall beside the fireplace or to set off the fireplace itself. At night, highlight the ornate molding around the ceiling or around a bay window. A highly polished parquet floor should not be lost in the shadows. Look around your home and, if there is some particular feature that you're especially proud of, imagine it illuminated by a special cast of light.

## WHY LIGHT?

There are three basic reasons for lighting a room: to provide general illumination for the room itself, to focus light on a specific place for a given task or activity, and to create mood and atmosphere. Interesting room lighting

usually incorporates all three functions to some degree. General lighting tends to be bland, with the intention of approximating general daylight. Task lighting is bright and pinpointed. Mood lighting is calculated to produce dramatic, intimate, or eye-catching effects. Think of the rooms in your home as stage sets and look at each with the eye of a stage designer. How can you make bolder statements with light? What areas can use more illumination? Where can a splash of colored light produce a decorative effect?

## PUT LIGHT WHERE YOU NEED IT

Lighting should be one of the first things you consider when you move into a new house or apartment. Check the electrical outlets around the rooms. Don't let the location and number of outlets be determined by an architect of a generation or two ago who never

*Looking like exotic birds, clip-on lights solve the problem of illuminating small, difficult-to-reach areas, such as the back of a closet (left). A contemporary metal cone-shade attached above a hanging bulb suits this casual, minimally furnished studio apartment perfectly (above).*

Warm, personal letters are written easily by the light of this tiny table lamp with a ginger-jar base and a delicate, splatter-patterned shade. The lamp's colors blend with the surrounding decor, making it cozier and even less obtrusive (above).

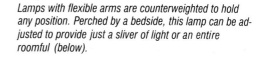

Lamps with flexible arms are counterweighted to hold any position. Perched by a bedside, this lamp can be adjusted to provide just a sliver of light or an entire roomful (below).

dreamed of the electronic world you would live in or of the number of activities that would engage you after the sun goes down. You should decide on what it is you want to illuminate. If there aren't enough outlets to let you put lights (not to mention other electrical equipment), where you want them, buy extension cords and adapter plugs.

The right adapter can increase the number of plugs an outlet will handle. You may also need a special adapter to handle flanged plugs and three-prong plugs. Be careful, however, not to overload the circuit.

A dimmer switch is one of the easiest ways to change the ambience of a room. Dimmer switches are neither ex-

pensive nor difficult to install. Almost every room can be enhanced at some time or other by having its overall lighting dimmed. Not only does a dimmer switch alter the mood of a room, but it cuts down on electricity and lowers utility bills. When it's time for you to move to another place, remove the dimmers and take them with you.

This Japanese-style bedroom is illuminated from above by a skylight and from below by a paper lantern. The paper lantern is part of a cord lamp attached to the ceiling. It can be raised or lowered as desired (above). A host of imaginative and entertaining light fixtures have been developed especially for high-tech and futuristic decors. The assortment here includes fluorescent light boards that can be hung anywhere, slender uplighters, and exciting table lamps (right).

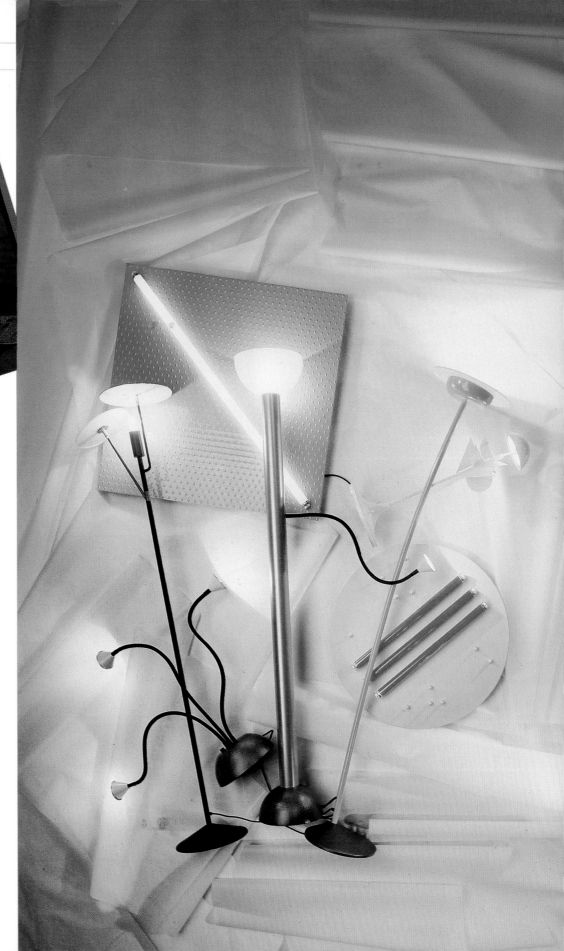

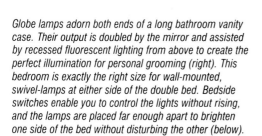

*Globe lamps adorn both ends of a long bathroom vanity case. Their output is doubled by the mirror and assisted by recessed fluorescent lighting from above to create the perfect illumination for personal grooming (right). This bedroom is exactly the right size for wall-mounted, swivel-lamps at either side of the double bed. Bedside switches enable you to control the lights without rising, and the lamps are placed far enough apart to brighten one side of the bed without disturbing the other (below).*

## CHOOSING THE RIGHT LAMP

The right lamp can function in several ways. Obviously, it is foremost a source of light, but the base and shade are also decorative components. The material and contour of the base, the color and shape of the shade, and the lamp's overall presence in a room become part of the general interior design. Some lamps even appear at first glance to be more sculptural or artistic than functional.

It's important that the lamp be the right size and shape for the area where it will be used. A lamp that is too large or too small will look out of place and work at cross purposes to your design plan. Similarly, the size and shape of the shade should be appropriately matched to the base of the lamp. Too large a shade makes the lamp look top-heavy, too small a shade will give the lamp a pinhead look.

Standard table lamps are widely available in classic styles that always look good: the cannister base, the candlestick shape, the tall slender column, and the squat ginger-jar style. You may, on the other hand, want to personalize a special spot with your own hand-crafted lamp. Almost any object can be turned into a table lamp. The basic lamp is simply a threaded pipe with washers and nuts at each end to hold the bulb socket and harp at the top and the base at the bottom. What encloses and conceals the threaded pipe is up to your imagination—bowls, cans, jars, wooden cylinders, tubing, ceramic figures. Just about anything that has a hollow interior or can be hollowed out can become a lamp base. Such objects as driftwood, stones, or other solid materials that are not hollow can still serve as lamp bases if you can insert or attach a bulb socket to the top and run the cord down the back.

Take an old lamp apart sometime and see for yourself how simple the basic construction is. Unplug the lamp first. Remove the shade and the bulb, then unscrew the nut at the base. You'll gradually feel the various parts at both ends of the lamp begin to loosen up. As they separate, take them apart and remember the order they were in so you can put the lamp back together again without leaving anything out. This procedure can be used to replace worn-out sockets or to rewire a lamp. A three-way socket can be installed to replace a one-way socket if you would like to be able to adjust the brightness of a table lamp. When you realize how easy it is to rewire an old lamp, you may find yourself considering lamps in second-hand stores and antique shops more seriously. There really are some good buys if you aren't intimidated by unattractive lamp shades and frayed wiring.

Pendant lamps that hang from the ceiling can also be constructed from various containers, such as cans, funnels, tubular paper, or Japanese lantern shades. Basically, the homemade pendant lamp is a light socket with a shade around it on the end of a hanging cord. To make one, turn off the electrical power at the control box and remove the present overhead fixture. Attach a new cord of the length that you want the pendant lamp to hang. Slip the bottom end through the new shade, then wire a one-way or three-way socket to the new cord.

Floor lamps are more versatile than they've been given credit for. Traditionally, they have sat close to a wall near a chair without a table lamp. But there's no rule that says the floor lamp must be bound to reading duty near a chair. It doesn't even have to stand against the

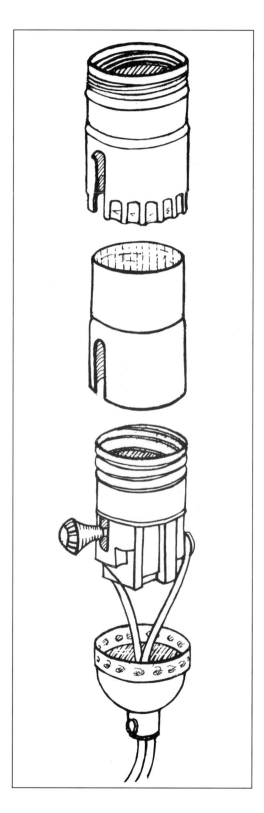

wall; a furniture arrangement in the center of the room could use a floor lamp if there isn't room for a table. And why not place a floor lamp next to a table? There's no reason to take up valuable table space with a lamp if it could be put to better use for sculpture, cut flowers, a plant, or books. Run the wire under a couch or rug or along a room divider. Some floor lamps have a swing arm that makes them ideal for a variety of purposes at once, such as illuminating a card table, then a couch.

The torchere-style floor lamp (called that because of its torch-like shape) casts light straight up, to bounce off the ceiling and fall back into the room with a gentle, diffused glow. For a room without an overhead light in the ceiling, a torchere lamp can approximate the general lighting usually received from the ceiling light. A torchere lamp is also a good choice when you want a subdued version of ceiling-lamp light.

The pharmacy floor lamp, with its bent gooseneck, casts strong light di-

*Whimsical neon provides atmospheric lighting in this room. Even the phone and the radio on the table contribute to the ambience (above). This diagram showing the parts of a standard lamp fixture reveals how easy it is to do your own repairs and rewirings (left). Cool and slim, this modern torchere-style floor lamp has a matching base and shade that give it the look of a freestanding column (facing page).*

rectly beneath it for reading or for working at a table. If the height is adjustable, lower it below eye level for quiet conversation or when you want a change in mood. Unobtrusive with its small, metal half-dome shade, the pharmacy lamp can fit into many decors.

If you have a high-tech design, consider using flexible-arm lamps, usually associated with drafting tables and office desks. They swing 360 degrees and can be adjusted to any height. What's more, by turning the shade, you can throw light up a wall or across the ceiling. Mounted on the wall or on a table beside a bed, a flexible arm lamp makes a handy reading light at night. At other times, shine it on the ceiling for general illumination or bend it lower than the height of the bed for accent or when watching television in bed.

## DRAMATIC LIGHTING EFFECTS

One of the most revolutionary lighting developments in recent years has been the use of track and cannister lighting in private homes. Formerly found only in art galleries and department stores or on the stage, these lighting fixtures have now become part of modern home decor. Being able to focus a strong beam of light on a particular spot or object in a room lets you truly use light as a design factor in ways never possible before. A cannister fixture behind a couch, for example, can send a spray of light up a wall. With colored filters you can change the light to match or complement other colors in the room or to fit a seasonal or holiday theme. A grated filter will cast

*Track lighting, usually mounted on the ceiling, works as effectively when mounted on the wall. Handsome cylinder shades open at both ends to cast light on three rows of kitchen decorations (above). A single undulating sheet of frosted plastic forms a sculptural lamp consisting of three concealed bays for fluorescent tubes (facing page).*

unusual shadows on the wall, as will a cannister lamp placed under or behind a large sprawling floor plant. And light coming from behind and between the foliage of a large plant creates a dramatic effect and displays the plant to its best advantage at night.

Track lights come in more than fifty styles that include variations in shape, size, color, and intensity. There are two types of track lights: those that are wired into the power source in the ceiling and those that are merely attached to the surface of the ceiling and plugged into an outlet somewhere else in the room. With the latter type, plan to run the cord so that it is as unobtrusive as possible, and runs the shortest distance across the ceiling.

Track lights aren't difficult to build yourself. Buy a length of electrical strip. Construct an L-shaped bracket to encase the strip, and paint it the color of the ceiling or stain it to match other wood tones in the room. Attach it to the ceiling with screws. Then attach flexible plug-in sockets into the outlets in the electrical strip. Buy minispot bulbs and screw each into a socket. Then run the cord across the ceiling to the nearest electrical outlet.

A row of track lights can be put to many uses. You can aim them in any direction to illuminate particular objects in the room, such as a piece of sculpture, a painting on the wall, a plant, a conversation area, or a bookcase. One lamp can be washing a wall in a soft pastel color while another is casting intriguing shadows on the floor beneath a leafy plant. Some models permit you to turn individual lights on and off as you need them. One spot may be turned off while another is aimed over the shoulder of someone reading in a nearby easy chair.

If you don't want to invest in a complete set of track lights, consider buying

*Two lines of minispots hung from a ceiling track—one long and one short—delineate the walls in this large loft space. A single low-hanging spot emphasizes the main gathering place (facing page). Rim-mount track lamps burn brighter and last longer than standard incandescent lamps and allow for precise beam control (right).*

portable minispots. These come in decorative colors and various styles. Some are freestanding, others attach to the wall, and some clamp on the edges of tables or bookcases. They are handy when you want to create a dramatic effect for the evening in one part of the room. A spot with a special framing projector regulates the shape and size of the pool of light so that it can be adjusted to fit the shape and size of the object on which it is directed, such as a painting or wall hanging.

However you decide to organize and personalize your home, don't leave lighting decisions to the last minute. With the wide assortment of lamps, fixtures, and even bulbs available today, there are plenty of options for enhancing the other design elements in your home with the exciting effects that only light can produce.

# DECORATIVE TOUCHES

## COLLECTIONS AND DISPLAYS

**D**ecorating with collections and arranging odd items for display is a fun way to personalize your home. It guarantees that your home design will be different from others. It puts your personal stamp on a room and makes guests feel that they are sharing your world, not just the space you happen to be living in.

## COLLECTIONS

There are four types of collections: conscious collections, unrecognized collections, collections of necessity, and theme collections. You may already have one or more of these types and could put them to good use in organizing and personalizing your home.

Conscious collections are those items that you know you collect—art objects, animal figures, posters, plants, whatever. You add on to them whenever you find a new one that intrigues you or when you can afford an addition or a new piece.

Unrecognized collections are those assortments of similar items that you have been accumulating over the years but never considered a real collection worthy of display: old scissors, caps, ties, purses, photographs (everyone has a drawer of them somewhere), salt and pepper shakers, wooden spoons, pillows, and so forth. All that may be needed is to take them from wherever you are accustomed to hiding them, arrange them in one place, perhaps purchase a few more, and begin to treat these items like a bona fide collection. Individually, they may have little or no

artistic merit, but collectively they may make an eye-catching or thought-provoking display. It's an inexpensive way to fill up a wall or give character and personality to a room.

The collections of necessity are those that you can't really dispense with, collections that just continue to grow no matter how you try to weed them out: books, records, cassettes, magazines, and the like. What to do with them? Consider them bona fide collections. The fact that they accumulate over the years proves that they have indeed become a collection, for you have collected them. So treat them as such and find a special place for them in a room where they would make logical and artistic sense. Put them on display. Even stacks of old magazines can create the right atmosphere for a study or den if arranged

*A mixture of frequently used bottles, mugs, and pitchers stored in front of a window serves double duty as a shimmering collection (left). A lucite display case permits a full view of colorful collectibles and interacts pleasingly with a sealed-off doorway in the background (above).*

*A cleverly contrived triple layer of collections—paintings, objets d'art, and books—offers a sumptuous feast for the eyes (above). Primitive sculpture seems appropriately housed in the deep, shadowy recesses of a ceiling-to-floor display unit in this room designed by Miles J. Lourie. Glass doors offer security as well as a dust-free environment. On a board above the couch, intriguing wooden and metal mechanical parts provide an interesting counter-study of abstract forms (right).*

neatly (or even with a studied shabbiness) in their proper corner of the room. To highlight them, paint sections of shelves different colors as a way to keep different types of magazines or records organized.

A thematic collection is little more than a theme or motif for a room or series of rooms: railroadiana, Americana, sports, theater, Native American art and artifacts or those from some other ethnic group, and so on. For example, an entire room or series of rooms can be decorated with Navajo fabrics and rugs, native artwork, pottery, sculpture, even photographs and posters. Or a sports motif can be developed from actual sporting equipment mounted on the walls (skis, rackets, skates, hunting or camping paraphernalia), framed covers of sports magazines, newspaper headlines, Olympic posters, and so forth. Theater or ballet items might include a clutter of old ticket stubs arranged on cork board, posters, actors' photos, scripts, reviews, director's chairs, or make-up lights. Whatever your interest or hobby, consider it from the point of view of providing decorative items for a room or a whole apartment and see what you come up with.

# THE ART OF DISPLAY

There are three major components of any display setting: location, background, and lighting.

The first decision is whether display items will be clustered in one place or arranged throughout a larger area.

There are advantages to both. If you collect art objects, you may want them gathered in one place so they can be admired in relation to each other. Having them in one place is also safer. People know where they are and can treat them carefully. Scattered around the room, expensive items can create a feeling of uneasiness in people not familiar with the room. When you look for the right space for your collection or display, consider every corner and nook in the room. Spaces that are not large enough for other furniture or activities are often just right for mounting or displaying your collections.

Some collections, however, look good scattered around. This is true of collections of animals made from all types of materials, or any other collection where quality is not important but quantity is. Many people have totemistic collections, those of favorite animals, such as pigs, owls, unicorns, or whales. Usually these animal motifs pop up on pillows, posters, napkins,

*Beloved objects are casually assembled to lend interest to a special storage alcove (below). Wondrous treasures are stored inside the meticulously labelled drawers of an antique oak storage chest (right).*

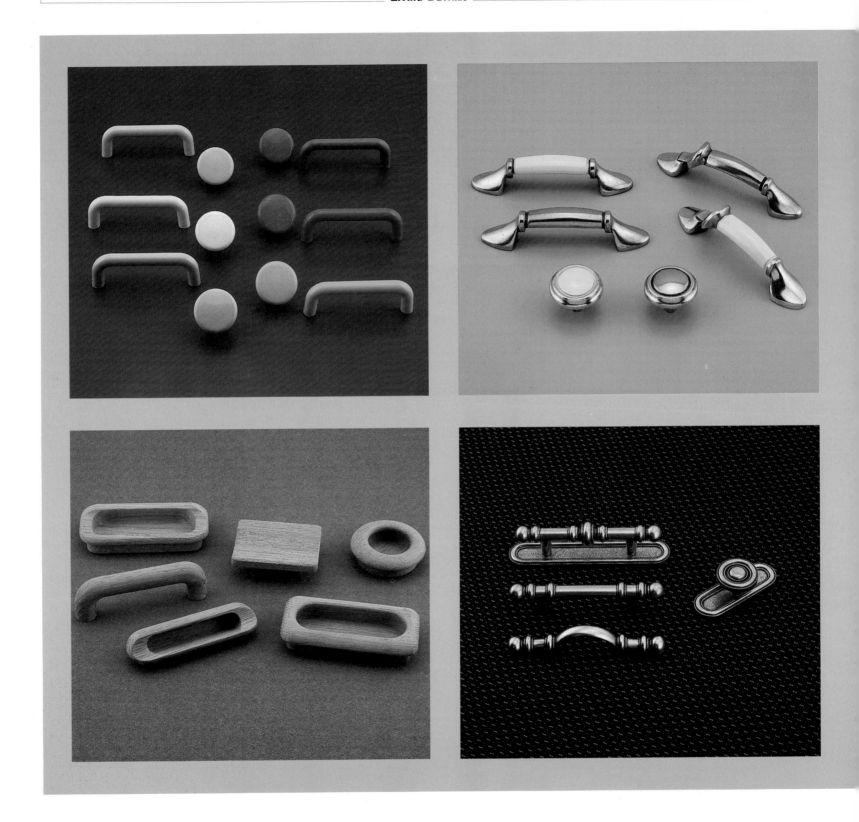

# DECORATIVE HARDWARE

An easy way to accent a room or area is to replace dull handles, knobs, and pulls with more exciting decorative hardware. You can either buy new ones or repaint the present ones so that they stand out from the pieces on which they are mounted. Hardware and home decorating stores have an enormous assortment of pulls and knobs in different colors, styles, and materials. Sometimes all it takes is new hardware to spruce up doors, cabinets, drawers, windows, even sinks. Don't overlook hinges in your design, either. They too can be painted to match the handles or knobs. Decorative hardware can help match pieces of furniture that are not really of similar styles. A chest of drawers and a desk in a bedroom, for example, may not be similar, but with the same drawer knobs painted the same color you can begin to unify the room.

curtains, and on mantle pieces and coffee tables. In fact, using an animal totem in this way can create a decorative motif for an entire room.

There are two ways you can display all your collected items in one place. You may want to arrange them with care and precision, especially if they are rare or expensive. You may even decide to buy or build a glass case in which to enclose them. On the other hand, a "confused clutter" is also an interesting way of gathering collected objects together. The montage or collage approach of a bowl of shells or a basket of pretty stones, for example, invites guests to hunt and search through the collection to see what's really there. It expresses an easy-going relationship with your collection and makes the room more comfortable, inviting, and less formal.

The background of a display setting is important. Color and material both can add or detract from the objects themselves. If you collect glass figurines or bottles, for example, glass shelves may not provide the most striking setting for them. On the other hand, wooden or ceramic objects may stand out more prominently on glass shelving. You may even want to put a mirror behind the shelves so objects can be seen from behind as well. Consider, therefore, the material and its texture before building shelves or cases. Wood, metal, glass, or fabric all have their special properties and should be selected to enhance the collection, not camouflage or detract from it.

Choose the color for the background carefully, whether you are painting the inside of shelving or the wall behind it. Note what color, if any, dominates your collection and choose an appropriate color for the background, one that will highlight the objects or set them apart from the backdrop. Don't hesitate to paint or paper a wall behind a collection a different color than the rest of the room, especially if your collection is mounted. This will make a strong statement about the importance of your display and give a specialness to the part of the room in which it is located.

Strategic lighting may be crucial for displaying your collections to their best advantage. Some objects, such as glassware or glossy ceramic pieces, look best during the day in natural light. Locate them near a window and they will sparkle. For obvious reasons, plants also need to be located near sources of daylight. At night you may want to illuminate plants or glass objects from behind or cast miniature spotlights on them. If you're building a case for a collection, install lighting so that even during the day the inside of the display case can be illuminated. Track lights focused on paintings or posters can be turned on when you want to call attention to them and switched off when you want a less dramatic effect in the room. Whatever you display, don't let poor lighting prevent your collected items from being a viable part of your overall design.

## A GALLERY OF PHOTOGRAPHS

Old photographs can make an interesting gallery in many types of rooms. Paint all the frames the same color or similar hues. Or let the uniqueness of each frame bring variety to the display. A gallery can consist of family photos or pictures of friends and places you've been. Or hunt in antique shops for old photos, posters, prints, and daguerreotypes of other families or scenes.

A photo collection concentrated in a single location need not be monotonous. Family photos are intermixed with compatible decorations on both a wall and a bureau top (left). Two different photo arrangements—one formal, using similar frames; and the other informal, using diverse frames—are juxtaposed on perpendicular walls (above, top). An inventive mounting provides a refreshing contrast in shape and color (above, bottom).

*Placed on shelves across a large window, these plants offer the perfect center section for an entire wall of collectibles (left). Mingling cut flowers with plants in a mantel basket allows for a constantly changing floral display (right). An indoor jungle is a romantic and adventurous addition to any home. The jungle effect in this sunny nook is created by grouping hanging plants with plants set behind large rocks on the floor (below). A well-lit row of plants makes a lively border along the base of a stairway (below, right).*

If you don't want to drive nail holes into the wall for each picture, mount a narrow three-to-four-inch shelf, with a lip, on the wall and rest your framed photos on it. The lip will keep them from sliding off. The advantage of this arrangement is that you can change the photos as you grow tired of them or keep them keyed to the seasons or holidays. A narrow shelf of photos can enliven a space that is otherwise difficult to decorate except with a wall hanging. It is particularly useful over a kitchen table, in a hallway or small alcove, or on a bend in the wall. Mounted and framed magazine covers, playbills, posters, or maps can be used in this way, too.

## PLANTS AND FLOWERS

Many people keep a few plants; some people live in veritable jungles. Either way, all it takes to create a unique setting for plants is to build special shelves or counters and illuminate them appropriately. Often, clustering plants in one end of a room (which may be done anyway to take advantage of natural light) can give the room character and purpose. A simple shelf across the top of double-hung windows will accommodate small pots. Larger ones can be hung from the ceiling.

Mirrors placed behind plants that are along interior walls will reflect light and openness and simultaneously create the impression that you have more plants than you actually do.

Expand your growing area outdoors with window boxes planted in the spring with summer flowers. When autumn arrives, you can change them to hardier flowers that will live into the cooler months. Window boxes come in plastic, metal, clay, and redwood that weathers to a neutral gray tone. Window boxes can also be painted to match or complement the color of your window treatments. Remember that you'll need a sturdy window ledge that is wide enough to hold a box and solid enough to handle the weight, which may double when filled with wet soil. If you live in an apartment, check with your landlord to make sure you can have window boxes.

Along with potted plants, you may want to include cut flowers as part of your overall design. While a vase of cut flowers can add color and beauty to almost any location, you might want to determine a special place where you regularly display flowers, changing them with the season or the occasion. On the mantel over a fireplace, on a small table in an unused alcove, on one end of a book shelf, or any similar location can become a special setting reserved only for the flowers you select to play a key role in your design.

When all is said and done, when all is painted and arranged, the personal statement made by any room depends on what of yourself you have put into the room. By displaying and sharing treasures and interests that mean the most to you, you can transform an ordinary room into a special place in your life. You'll enjoy the room more, and others will feel that by being there they've come to know you better.

# KITCHEN AND BATHROOM

## THE KITCHEN

**W**hen you move into a new home or apartment, all the rooms look unplanned except two: the kitchen and the bathroom. Whereas the other rooms are filled only with expectation, the kitchen and bath seem already on their way to being furnished, the plans already drawn. Obviously, the determinants in this situation are the appliances and fixtures that come with a living space. And even were you to bring in your own kitchen appliances, plumbing and gas lines are already laid out for you. Although the options are fewer, the challenge of making these rooms work your way is more exciting.

By necessity, most people spend more time in their kitchens than in any other room. Not only are meals prepared and shared there, but many people settle down in the kitchen between meals to attend to other activities: reading, writing letters, paying bills, playing cards, even just visiting with friends who drop by. If you're fortunate to have a large roomy kitchen, you can intentionally organize it to accommodate other non-kitchen activities. If yours is a small kitchen, such as a galley kitchen, your best bet is simply to organize it well for preparing meals; there's not much else you can do in it.

A large eat-in kitchen is a real find for apartment dwellers whose actual living space is usually quite limited. A large kitchen usually has enough room for work areas and storage, and if there isn't enough to begin with, you can often construct your own. There may even be room for an eating area pleasant enough for entertaining guests, as well as for quick breakfasts and lunches. What's more, a large spacious kitchen will let you control traffic patterns so that other family members can use it and pass through it without getting in the way of the cook.

Let's take a look at the three considerations of kitchen design in some detail: work and storage areas, room for other functions such as dining, and control of traffic flow.

Ideally, you should have counter tops near both the stove and the sink. If the ones that come with your kitchen are

*Vinyl-coated wire mesh fits into any kitchen wall area to form a versatile storage rack. Hooks can be moved to accommodate countless arrangements of cookware and utensils (facing page). A wall of adjustable shelves and attractive, transparent canisters in various sizes allows you to display the interesting colors and shapes of foodstuffs (above).*

*When not in use, kitchen utensils mingle successfully with decorated plates, herbs, and dried flowers. Brass, copper, and iron implements, in particular, harmonize well with appliances (facing page). A handsome wooden slat-screen slides down to cover these kitchen shelves when they are not in use (left). A cluster of copper pots and pans, hanging over the sink like exotic metal foliage, offers visual relief in this all-white kitchen. It also provides a linear balance for the track lighting (below).*

not adequate and there isn't space nearby to construct counter tops, an island work area is the next best thing. By locating the island counter a few feet from the stove and sink, you will create a work triangle between sink, counter top, and stove. In a well-planned kitchen, the refrigerator is close by so you don't have to walk far to get food. Within the triangle, you can wash vegetables, rinse meats, cut them up, and begin cooking them on the stove with a minimum of steps. The work island also directs traffic flow around the area where you'll be working. Most people passing through the kitchen will respect the space behind the island as the cook's domain.

A work island can be as compact or as elaborate as you choose. Some are permanently situated, others are on castors and can be rolled to where they are needed. A work island usually has storage space underneath and will sometimes even have a shallow counter for quick meals. An island with a butcher block top is multifunctional and especially easy to prepare meals on and clean up afterwards.

If you don't have room for a work island, consider buying a large cutting board that will fit over the sink. You'll be able to rinse food, cut it up, and toss the cuttings in the garbage disposal or trash can without taking a step. When the board is not needed, slide it back onto the drainage counter or store it behind a door or in a closet.

You may want to define the work space with a screen rather than with a centrally located table or work island. A screen has the advantage of concealing unsightly clutter from the dining area. A folding screen can be secured to the floor with angle irons, so it won't tip over. After it's secured, you can line its inner side with peg board and use it for hanging cookware or other utensils.

Large iron hooks hung from a beam hold baskets and basketfuls. Metal baskets come in many different sizes and styles and make good-looking storage units whether sitting on a shelf or suspended from the ceiling (below). Fill an open area under a laundry room counter with vinyl-coated wire baskets and you have an efficient linen closet (left). This little corner presents an intriguing combination of wet bar and study that works surprisingly well. Don't be afraid to use the niches that you have to accommodate seemingly disparate activities. With a little careful planning, the results are sure to please you (right).

When organizing storage areas, keep in mind that work always proceeds more easily when what you want is where you need it. For example, try to store detergents, cleansers, mops, and brushes near the sink. Cookware should be close to the stove, and dishes near the dining or serving area. Similarly, utensils are handiest in drawers or hanging near the work areas where they will be used.

Cookware and many other cooking utensils can be attractively displayed out in the open, so don't feel you must hide it away in drawers or cupboards. Polished copper or bright enamel colors can contribute to an overall color scheme. Simple hooks on the wall behind the stove will hold pots and pans where they can be conveniently reached when you need them. Another alternative is to suspend them from the ceiling. Either screw a length of one-by-two-inch board to the beams in the ceiling and attach hooks along it, or screw an appropriately painted straight ladder to the ceiling beams and hang S-hooks from the rungs. The ladder arrangement lets you hang a wealth of cookware and utensils and provides options for organizing them.

Equally handy are wicker baskets or vinyl-covered wire baskets and bins suspended from the ceiling for storing small items, such as vegetables, sponges, linens, catfood, or paper products. Older kitchens with high ceilings have a number of storage possibilities above your head: shelves, racks, hooks, and any combination of them. Look above you and let your imagination find ways to use this space.

If a window in the kitchen doesn't have a view worth preserving, consider building a shelf across it. It can be used for spices, plants, or glassware. A glass shelf will allow more light through than a wooden one, and will actually help to conceal the unsightly view.

Another unusual arrangement is to store spices on the bottom of a shelf instead of on top of it. Simply glue the screw-on caps to the underside of a shelf and screw the jar up into it. Shop around for an antique or designer set of spice jars, or interesting glass ones, and fill them with the spices you use.

Since the kitchen is a place of diverse activities, it should have modular lighting. Appropriate lighting can make or break a kitchen, both in terms of aesthetics and of utility. Uniform lighting from one overhead source centrally located in the ceiling not only creates a dull aura, but it is usually hard on the eyes. The ideal lighting arrangement is a combination of general lighting and task lighting. General lighting is used when no specific activity is going on. Task lighting is focused on specific areas to illuminate them for specific tasks. It is easier and much more enjoyable, for example, to prepare a meal when there is direct light on the work areas and the stove. One spot that needs variable lighting is the dining area. For quiet, romantic meals, you'll want subdued lighting, but bright light

is necessary for other activities such as writing, reading, sewing, playing games, or working at a hobby.

Also, consider the use of light to distinguish and define areas in a large kitchen or a loft space where only one area is the actual kitchen. While it's true that area rugs, different wall coverings, or a change in the paint color can distinguish different areas within a larger space, lighting provides the most distinct definitions. Low lights sprayed against the wall behind the dining table, for example, will state clearly that this area is separate and distinct from the less-dramatically lit work spaces. A corner of the kitchen used as a home office or hobby spot could be lit with track lights so that it comes alive when the rest of the kitchen is dark.

In general, a pleasant kitchen is one that can match many moods. Track lighting, small wall lamps, and high-intensity lamps can direct bright light where you need it, and dimmer switches on overhead lights and those near the dining area will let you modulate the intensity when you wish. If your overhead light looks like it's a leftover from a bygone and best-forgotten era, replace it with a more modern fixture that suits your personality. A new hanging light fixture over the table can transform an entire kitchen. Store the old one and replace it before you move, taking yours with you, of course.

Of all the rooms in the home, the kitchen is often the most fun to decorate since it contains so many odds and ends, both practical and aesthetic. In fact, often the two can't be distinguished. Unlike other rooms, the kitchen can welcome clutter and turn it into a warm, homey style all its own. In a busy kitchen, an honest display of eclecticism can pull together the myriad of utensils and gadgets that are needed for turning out meals.

Keep in mind that however you organize it and decorate it, the kitchen is primarily a room where you share your life with those close to you. Like it or not, you cannot keep "life" from happening in the kitchen. First and foremost, your kitchen should be a warm, comfortable, welcoming place that you enjoy being in.

## THE BATHROOM

There is relatively little furniture in the bathroom; the fixtures are impersonal and, as their name suggests, fixed; and the smallness of the room prevents bold personal statements. In most tile bathrooms, even the wall space where you can create your own decorative theme is limited to what extends above the tile.

When you are deciding how to decorate your bathroom, you might want to consider a better-quality wallpaper. Because the square footage is relatively small, the cost is not as prohibitive as in another room. The same is true of paint. Forget the standard antique white of so many apartment bathrooms and investigate more interesting colors. Top the paint job off with a toilet seat and towel racks of a matching or complementing color.

You might choose to be bold and original when it comes to your bathroom walls. For example, they could easily be papered with magazine covers, headlines from newspapers, pin-ups, or old maps. Paste them on and smooth them down with a straightedge, and then give them two coats of polyurethane to keep them from yellowing, being soiled, or blistering from condensation and humidity.

Traditionally, a bathroom is pulled

Carefully placed pictures and light fixtures, combined with a soothing pastel color scheme, give this bathroom a distinctly elegant appearance (above). A two-tone color scheme involves every feature of this playfully warm bathroom (left). This bathroom is pulled together by a sprightly print repeated in the upper wall, window curtain, sink curtain, and chair seat (facing page).

together by coordinated towels, bathmat, and shower and window curtains. You'll probably do the same.

If the toilet seat is old and unexciting (as most of them are), shop around at bathroom boutiques and supply shops for a colored or wooden one. If you have artistic ability, buy a plain white seat and paint it yourself.

Storage in a bathroom usually presents a problem since not much space is devoted to closets or shelving. Most apartments have a linen closet near the bathroom, but still there is a need for storage space in the bathroom itself. In some bathrooms, the medicine cabinet and the area beneath the sink are about all there is. In bathrooms with older fixtures, the sink may be a wall-hung model without storage space underneath. You can construct your own by building shelves or stacking a couple of boxes or crates beneath it. Enclose them with a skirt attached around the sink. You might use the same material you used for the window curtains or the shower curtain.

Another wasted area in many bathrooms is the wall behind the bath tub. If the bath does not have a shower and is, therefore, not tiled, at least one good shelf could be built there to hold soap, shampoo, bath oil, and face cloth. You may even want to keep a supply of books and magazines on it for reading sessions while you soak. Rig up a little reading lamp on the shelf, but be sure it is well secured and in no danger of falling into the tub. If you don't need to store many accessories on the shelf, reserve part of it for decorative items. A piece of sculpture or even a simple flowering plant can lend some flair to the bath environment. You might consider extending the shelving all the way up the wall behind the tub to accommodate most of your spare towels and toilet articles.

Remember that non-bathroom furniture can be adapted attractively into the bathroom. In a large bathroom, it is sometimes possible to find room for a chest of drawers, a bureau, or even a book case. When you roam through second-hand furniture shops, keep your bathroom in mind and look for pieces that would fit in. A clothes tree or a plain pole with hooks is handy for changing clothes or hanging towels. A hanging wire basket can be filled with toilet articles or first-aid supplies.

No one likes to groom himself or herself in front of a poorly lit mirror. The bathroom mirror should be brightly illuminated. If your bathroom has a single overhead fixture that casts unbecoming shadows on your face, consider removing the fixture, running wire down each side of the mirror, and installing two wall lamps on either side to give full-faced illumination without shadows. Or install light panels with bare bulbs down each side of the mirror, such as those used in back-stage dressing rooms. Soft, low-wattage bulbs will give a more flattering light than brighter light bulbs.

To see yourself better in the bathroom, you can hang a full-length mirror, either vertically to see your entire body or horizontally at chest level. Mirrored tiles, described in Chapter 4, can be arranged either as one large mirror or in a fractured pattern. If there is not much natural light in the room, mirrors placed across from the window will create an open, airy dimension on interior walls. Of course, you may want to go the opposite route and install smoked or tinted mirrors to add a touch of shadow and mystery.

Another area that can usually benefit from the effect of mirrors is the tub. A frieze of mirror tiles on the wall around the edge of the tub will catch color and light in an area of the bathroom where

*Bathroom shelving of stylish chrome and fine-wired glass works well in a small, high-tech bathroom. Here, a mirror-and-shelf combination, two different types of shelving units, and a chrome trolley offer ample surface storage area without appearing bulky or shadowy (above, top). This single shelf mounted on the wall above the towel rack represents a traditional way of providing lots of additional bathroom storage in little space. Single hooks, such as the one on which the robe hangs, and a shelf surrounding the tub at rim level are equally efficient space-savers (above, bottom).*

*A bathroom is typically the tiniest room in the house and resists conventional decorating tricks. Sometimes the temptation to turn it into a unique ''theme'' room is irresistible and, in the end, pays off. A humorously rustic bathroom includes barn-like wall slats, a barrel sink, a horse-collar mirror frame, and a plow-handle towel rack. A large print of a country scene completes the motif (left). The visual effect of this bathroom is all that counts. With books embedded in plaster, a faux marble toilet, and marbelized wallpaper, you'll see that it's not hard—and lots of fun—to create a distinctive bathroom in the tiniest space (right).*

there usually is none. It will also open up the space around you when you take a bath, eliminating the claustrophobic feeling that clings to many bath tubs located along a wall or recessed into an alcove.

If you sometimes wash laundry in the sink and need a place to dry it, construct a permanent clothesline over the tub. Above the showerhead and the tile, attach a piece of one-by-four-inch board at each end of the tub. Eye screws placed at intervals will let you run clothesline back and forth for at least four or five lengths. After taking the dry clothes down, remove the line and store it until you need it next.

Complete your laundry facility with a compact ironing center, a wall-hung unit that contains the ironing board, electrical outlet, hot-iron storage compartment, and even a spotlight in case you have to hang the unit in a dark corner of the room. Some models are recessed into the wall and others are surface-mounted on wall studs, perfect for apartment dwellers. When the ironing board is folded up, Murphy-bed fashion, the entire compartment extends only a few inches out from the wall and looks no different than a typical cabinet. This unit may also fit into a corner of the kitchen.

The trend in bathroom renovation today is to turn the bathroom into a real health and relaxation center. Of course, if you don't plan to live in your present home for very long, you won't want to make serious alterations. Nevertheless, in small ways you can touch up the bathroom so that it is an inviting and restful room to spend time in.

# TWENTY-ONE LOOKS AND WHY THEY WORK

Some decorating schemes work and others don't. One plan seems natural, as if it belongs in a given space; another is a misfit, peculiar, out of place. Even the most expensive improvements can turn out wrong. Conversely, the simplest, least costly addition can often finish off a room just the way you want it to. Ultimately, there are no guarantees that by following all the rules of home design, a room or apartment will come together. The rules are merely guidelines, time-tested suggestions for you or your designer to incorporate and use as long as they work for you. In the final analysis, you must please yourself within the physical limitations of your lifestyle.

The following gallery of photographs shows decorating schemes that might work well for people with rented homes or limited budgets. They have been chosen because they exemplify decorating ideas that can be adapted within narrower parameters of cost, time, portability, and amount of use. Use these rooms as models and inspiration for yourself or for your designer. As you browse through them, notice the effects they achieve; how they use space, color, design, and texture; and how they create a mood. Also notice what you don't like, and try to understand why it doesn't please you. Even though these looks have worked well for someone else, parts of them may not work for you, so adapt what you like to your own situation.

Remember, your living space is your own. Only you know the needs and desires it must fulfill to make you feel most comfortable. Perfecting the living details—the elements of organization, structure, and decoration—to your own style and demands will transform your house or apartment into a home.

*S*ome people use plants as simple decorative touches—to add a spot of greenery, to fill an empty place on a shelf or table. Other people, however, take full advantage of a southern exposure and a corner studded with windows to create a veritable solarium. The designers have done so here to create a room bursting with vegetation. All the furnishings are in keeping with the outdoor garden motif. White wicker patio furniture is upholstered with green and yellow material to convey a bright, breezy springtime feeling.

Instead of impeding the sunlight with curtains or blinds on these four corner windows, framed panes of glass are hung in front of the actual windows. On one side are leaded glass panes that mysteriously distort the images seen through them without diluting the full sunlight. Over the love seat are two beautiful stained glass panels that add variety and color to a room dominated by white, yellow, and green. Both sets of decorative panes provide an element of privacy if needed.

When decorating with numerous plant arrangements, you need not invest in expensive pots and containers or take excruciating care in placing the plants. In a room where the garden effect draws the eye to the plants themselves, traditional clay pots and baskets suffice and the arrangement can be more haphazard. When presenting a natural look, a single plant on the floor at the corner of the love seat looks just right. So do the others hanging from the ceiling; sitting on tables, counters, and window sills; and standing unabashedly on the floor.

*A* large open space such as the one seen here could be transformed into many different looks. Consider how the room would look devoid of all furnishings, and then let your eye replace each element, color, and decorative touch one by one. The combination of colors and fixtures creates a gentle, feminine sensibility.

The baby grand piano is located in the far end of the room, made brighter by a mirror reflecting the windows in the opposite end of the room and providing extra light for the piano player. To increase the light even more, mirror panels have been added to the back of the door and on the opposite wall.

A ballet barre along one wall suggests that practice sessions are actually held in the room, yet the couch, coffee table, and sitting area across from it suggest other uses. The lively art of ballet is reflected in the open wire cubes dancing over the piano and the vibrant design of the area rug. Even the graceful swirls of the throw pillows echo the smooth liquidity of the art. The geometry of form and movement is also seen in the multiple shapes used as bases for the glass-topped coffee table.

The two futon couches have simple lines and a neutral color tone that blends in with the walls and floor. Their smooth forms and light colors keep the room airy looking and add a delicate touch where such pieces are usually large and imposing instead. Dashes of blue and pink in the pillows and rug add a whisper of color to the otherwise monochromatic room. Overall, this comfortable room is carefully designed to subtly suggest the follow-through on a gentle, evocative theme.

**W**hat can you do with walls and a ceiling left rough and unfinished? How can you hide the framework when you aren't ready to put up the money to complete a converted garage or attic? How can you prevent lovely and elegant pieces of furniture from palling next to ugly, neglected walls? The answer is black. Black covers a multitude of mistakes and problems and creates·a spectacular foil or backdrop for more colorful and interesting items. In this room, a baby grand piano, a ceramic Buddha, a dramatic print from Florence, and a rug and a tapestry on the piano, both with wonderful geometric patterns, shine in their own glory for rough, neglected walls do not compete with them.

Painting the background of a room black inspires equally simple solutions to other decorating challenges. Play upon the unrefined feel of the room in small ways. How should large, sprawling spider plants be displayed? Hang them from the ceiling in rough ceramic pots with basic rope or twine. How to light the piano so music can be read and the right keys struck? Drop a naked bulb from the ceiling and conceal it with a paper lantern. How to display the Buddha? Set him on a wooden packing crate in front of a magnificent window unobstructed by lavish curtains or draperies, adorned only with inexpensive rolled bamboo shades. From top to bottom, the genius of this room is to use natural, unpretentious components to let the more exciting pieces speak for themselves. In fact the prized items here—literary, musical, and artistic—are like outposts of culture and civilization in an otherwise unimpressive environment.

*T*his sleeping alcove's coziness and appeal comes from an economical use of space and a charming combination of complementary materials. Since the brick walls and heavy-beamed ceiling are givens, the owner exploited the rustic look by decorating with other natural materials. First, the brick walls are painted white to contrast with the dark wooden ceiling and make the long narrow space feel light and open. A white pelt bedspread echoes the roughness of the walls and ceiling, while homemade country quilts hanging at the head and foot of the bed add warmth. Two bamboo shades can be lowered to close off the sleeping nook. For visual and textured continuity, the window shade is made of the same coarse natural fibers. Unlike solid curtains or drapes, the shades let light through during the day so that even when the shades are down, the room is not foreshortened.

The bed shown here is a simple platform bed built on a raised base. The space beneath makes a handy storage area, especially in a narrow room like this where a dresser or chest of drawers would add clutter. The carpeted extension on the first level provides extra seating. These simple strategies work to successfully minimize the bedroom effect of the room that can limit its adaptability as an entertaining area.

Complementary, portable, and adaptable furnishings such as shades and quilts are a strategic investment. The owner will be able to use them in the next home or apartment. The shades could cover windows, and the quilts might be thrown over couches or return to their more orthodox role on beds themselves.

*T*wo textures dominate this room: sleek, smooth blond pine wood and softly undulating folds of overstuffed pillows. Even the mattress and quilt hung to the side during the day become a vital component in the design concept.

When a floor is as finely finished as this one and the border trim of the room and windows is in good shape, leaving them exposed and unadorned creates a natural clean look. The bamboo shades on each of the windows continues the wood tone motif and leaves the windows unobstructed. When the shades are pulled up, as on the side, leaded window panes are revealed, another structural feature of this room that should be seen, not hidden from view.

Contrasting with the comfortable plushness of the couch and its soft, inviting pillows is the plain straight-backed chair, providing another balance between the hard surfaces of wood and the cushiony softness of woven materials. A number of wicker baskets are placed throughout the room as decorative touches, complementing the shades and pine wood. They also serve as catchalls for magazines and other odds and ends.

Simple shelves built between the window frame and the back wall provide more structured storage space. The cluttered effect in the shelves is well thought-out and surprisingly successful. The cluttered, lived-in look (doubled by the use of mirrors) contrasts aesthetically with the untouched glossy surface of the floor.

Another useful storage area often overlooked is the space between the top of the window casement and the ceiling. Here a plank of shelving has been attached above each window to store items and display a collection of jars—a utilitarian and attractive trick.

One of the problems of living in a studio apartment is that one must tidy up after every activity to provide a clean environment for the next one. This is especially true of turning the bedroom into a pleasant living room each morning and then transforming it back into a bedroom again at night. If you live alone and are home by yourself most nights, you may choose to leave your sofa bed out rather than put it away every day. Yet you may not want to come home every night to a single room that looks like a makeshift bedroom. How to avoid this problem? Create an atmosphere of mock sumptuousness with a bohemian canopy made from sheets, pipes, and a couple of cans of paint.

Utilizing and also camouflaging the exposed pipes that run along the ceiling, the decorator of this room draped them with sheets—splattered with paint and shredded on the edges—and knotted them directly overhead. To complement the whimsically haphazard effect of this arrangement, the wall behind the bed was painted by gravity rather than with a brush. When the apartment is meant to be a bedroom, the sofa bed is left pulled out and the sheets are extended along the pipes to create the canopy effect. The cushions from the sofa are stacked at the foot of the bed to provide extra seating. To transform the room back into a living room, simply fold up the bed and push the sheets back against the wall.

The color scheme in the sheets and on the wall looks haphazard, but a discerning eye selected light blue as the dominant color tone, probably matching the comforter brought from a previous apartment. Brightly colored pillows tossed on the bed emphasize the ''merry prankster'' design on the wall, as does an ordinary spotlight clamped to one of the overhead pipes.

*I*t makes perfect sense to match the structural materials of the room with furnishings of similar texture and color. The same principle holds for converting a basement, garage, or industrial space into a living space. To completely renovate would be costly and time-consuming. Instead use what is there to dictate what to add.

In this room, the overhead girders, supporting pillars, and spiral staircase are metal, so the decorators chose aluminum venetian blinds as the room divider. By pulling them up or leaving them lowered, partially opening them or closing them tightly, people can adjust the delineated areas to suit their activity needs.

To make rearranging the floor plan as easy as possible, use lightweight pillows and futons for couch, bed,

and chairs. When the central space is needed for entertaining or a family activity, the furniture can be moved aside. The television, as well, is located on a portable stand with castors so it can be rolled into the bedroom, left out in the main area, or pushed out of the way altogether when not in use.

A large room divided like this one is amazingly versatile—bedroom, playroom, tv room, and study all rolled into one. Daily demands on space change frequently and suddenly, and what better way to accommodate the many needs than to create a space that can be completely rearranged at any time. The sturdy aluminum fixtures are not as costly as constructing walls, and they can be transported easily to a new location.

138

*A*n apartment in an older home converted into rental spaces will sometimes have a bathroom converted from a former bedroom or sitting room. These large, roomy bathrooms are both fun and challenging to personalize. Often you can use them for related health activities, such as this bath complete with exercise bars and jump rope.

The large window is not obscured with curtains and, with slatted blinds as the only treatment, is a source of natural light. The clean lines of the casement match the molding and other woodwork in the room. The overhead lighting fixture has been replaced with a small spotlight aimed at the tub. The reflection in the metallic wallpaper provides additional, pleasingly diffuse light. Notice how the paper on one wall has effectively added a different color and pattern variation to the bone white room.

Shelving and concealed storage space that would detract from the basic lines of the room have been sacrificed to maintain openness. The decorator has opted for the cluttered look, leaving toilet articles and accessories exposed on the tub, tank, and shelf over the sink. The wooden end table at the foot of the tub is a good example of how a piece of furniture originally intended for another room can be adapted to a bathroom. The table nicely balances the floor-to-ceiling wooden exercise bars.

The throw rug at the sink is both decorative and useful. It accents the dark brown color of the wood tones elsewhere while at the same time protecting the wall-to-wall carpeting under the sink. Another important personal touch is the use of cut flowers, which indicates that the owner enjoys the decorative opportunities of the bath as well as its utilitarian purposes.

*O*ne can have fun and be adventurous while decorating a bathroom for a little boy or girl. Approach it with a playful point of view, trying to see it as your child might. Ask children what they would like in their own bathroom before you start, so you give them a sense of participation and help ensure them that you are creating a room they'll enjoy spending time in.

This bathroom is decorated in traditional pink and blue pastels with the delicate touches that appeal to a young girl's feminine sensibilities. Once you've decided on the basic color scheme, it's easy to match things like towels, cups, sponges, washcloths, tissues, mirror frames. As in a playroom, some toys and accessories can be left out in the open without detracting from the look of the room. In this room, extra storage space was created under the sink by attaching a skirt to it.

If you aren't inclined to put money into a lot of wallpaper for a look like this, you might try stenciling or sketching a mural on the walls. You don't need to be a skilled artist or muralist to come up with a good-looking room since the style should be childlike, whimsical, and primitive. The blue hearts on the wainscoting, the tulips over the tub, and the potted flowers could all be drawn and painted or stenciled for much the same effect as the wallpaper used in this example.

The clever window treatment is perfect for a bathroom setting. Only the lower half of the window needs to provide privacy, and is covered with latticework, repeating the pattern on the walls, and backed by a sheer curtain. The upper half is left open to provide light. The top of the casement is treated with a pink and blue swag delicately gathered at the ends and in the middle.

*I*f you dream of living in a large, stately Victorian house, you don't have to wait until you do to begin collecting Victoriana. While the Victorian look implies an interior cluttered with massive, heavy pieces of furniture, dark, somber colors, and a plethora of odds and ends and decorative items, a simpler Victorian flavor can be achieved with just a few period pieces and Victorian accessories in any open and light room. The old-fashioned look achieved is nostalgic without appearing affected or stodgy, forced or overdone.

In this sitting room, for example, an ornately carved lamp base with a fringed shade stands beside a bentwood rocker. These elements are all that are needed to evoke the Victorian era, but the dark-stained shutters filter the light for added antique flavor. Futhermore, they lend an air of solidarity and permanence to the window casements, which have been painted out by making them the same color as the walls.

Instead of a love seat or chaise lounge, a plain hammock fastened to wall studs lets one languish in the diffuse sunlight. When more unobstructed room is needed, the hammock can be taken down and stored in a cupboard or closet. The modern chrome light fixture hanging over the end of the hammock is positioned for comfortable reading and reminds one of the present era. Deep red cushions strewn on the floor encourage casual reclining, and the leafy plants and cut flowers add a fresh and open outdoor touch to an otherwise enclosed and proper interior. From top to bottom, this sitting room is an evocative, comfortable, and inviting niche.

*A* large room does not have to be lavishly furnished. A minimalist look allows a pleasant, streamlined effect without a lot of expense. The long blank wall behind the bed in this room is attractively broken up with a very small print, which, in its clean Spartan manner, completes the wall as adequately as a large print or even a grouping of several smaller prints would.

The success of the black-and-white color scheme in this bedroom is a result of the play between the strongly contrasting tones. A setting of one dark color accenting a basically white room is easy to arrange because it re-quires only a few well-placed objects incorporating the strong color—in this case, pillow cases, a comforter, and the small print. In fact, too many jet black items would destroy the clean, unspoiled look of this room.

Despite the minimal number of furnishings, this room contains ample concealed storage space. The two matching chests of drawers are modular units that are easily added onto when the need for more storage space arises. The platform bed is a self-contained storage unit with four drawers in the base and two on each side.

In a room where the bed must be placed along a wall, select a design that has two drawers the width of the bed that can be pulled out from the same side. Headboards for platform beds offer all kinds of various storage systems. One style consists of a large storage bin with a flip-up top that serves as a shelf for books or art objects. Other styles have several tiers of shelves.

The reading lamp next to the bed is high tech and fits in well with the sleek minimalist approach to decorating. It even harmonizes with the rowing machine, which along with any other exercise equipment can be left out without detracting from the overall look of the room.

In this quiet room of muted pink and blue, the focus is low near the floor, even inviting activity at floor level. The wide platform bed, although it takes up a good deal of floor space, is surprisingly unobtrusive. It becomes an area strewn with pillows that invites daytime lounging rather than a piece of furniture useful only at night. The futon against the wall is a perfect complement to the bed. Together they balance the room and provide plenty of space for overnight guests.

The low furniture suggests an Oriental flavor that has been consciously introduced by the large shoji screen that folds out behind the bed. In a large one- or two-room apartment, a screen such as this can adequately but beautifully divide the living and bedroom area from a kitchen and dining space.

Notice how the blue-gray color of the bed and couch is used as accent elsewhere—in the pillows, the painted molding and baseboards, and in the matting on the framed print. The stark black of the bowl, vase, and floor lamp provides a striking contrast to the dusty colors that dominate the room.

The torchère lamp is a graceful sculptural piece in itself, its clean lines boldly standing out against the unusual bend in the wall behind it. Unlike the standard-model floor lamp, the torchère casts all of its light toward the ceiling, where it diffuses to give more general illumination. The small Japanese screen beneath the print is lit from behind by a single bulb creating a soft glow of light and warmth low near the floor. In a quiet way, it echoes the effect created by the large shoji screen where each square panel tempers the light coming through it.

*O*ften when you move into an apartment or house, the rooms will have just been painted, usually in bone white. You may choose not to repaint, either because it would cost too much or because the present paint job is new, clean, and adequate. So you can offset the stark white with colorful furnishings, or you can go with the bone white and paint or buy furnishings to match it, as in this bright and lively room. The tables, chairs, shelving unit, couches—even the piano and stool—are the same white as the room. A few orange, black, and black-and-white patterned pillows; the books in the shelves; a colorful Picasso poster; and a basket of red flowers are all the touches of color needed to give accent and life to a potentially sterile-looking room. A few well-placed objects of color take on a larger role since color is rare and valuable to this overall minimalist theme.

The black-and-white area rug with the geometric design both brightens and draws together the room. The diminutive structure of the white parson's tables and director's chairs ensure that the central area does not look crowded or cluttered. Untreated windows add to the stark brightness and purity of the room. If light control and privacy are not an issue, an unbroken view into a green yard can contrast nicely with a room purposely devoid of lavish color.

Modular shelving provides storage space that complements the furniture in color and smooth unadorned surfaces. An open space is left beneath the three top shelves to enclose an upright piano. The cabinet doors next to it contain a television set and stereo equipment. Additional storage is found in the bank seating along the walls, where drawers are built into the base underneath.

*I*n a long sunlit apartment located on a high floor with a city view, take advantage of both the natural light and the panoramic view from the spacious windows. There's no need to hang curtains or drapes on the windows since privacy is not an issue. Besides, on a limited budget, the expense of treating such large windows could be prohibitive. Instead, venetian blinds will suffice to regulate light.

The floor plan of this studio apartment allows a direct view from the living room and kitchen area into the bedroom at the far end. Plants and a few pieces of furniture are used to separate the two major areas with a third area. The far edge of the living/entertainment space is delineated by a ceiling-high potted tree. The middle ''room'' is defined by a shelf near the ceiling that extends over both the small table used as desk and the dining table and is lined with vines. The two types of foliage suggest to the eye that there are two distinct zones here.

Similar pieces of furniture unify the middle ''room'' further: simple white formica-topped tables for desk and eating area, accompanied by two tan director's chairs. Although this apartment is large enough to accommodate substantial pieces of furniture, director's chairs are a prudent investment for apartment living because they can be folded up when not in use and stored out of the way. When used as permanent chairs, they are attractive yet unpretentious, relatively inexpensive, and available in a wide variety of colors.

The love seat and chair are positioned to take advantage of the panorama and block the view into the bedroom. The glass-topped coffee table lets light through and reflects it, adding to the airy ambience. A large mirror hung over the bed also adds airiness and depth to the small bedroom area and reflects the plants from the other room—a clever way to add a touch of greenery to a room too small to sustain plants of its own.

*I*f a room or apartment has at least one great asset, such as an impressive fireplace, a well-kept hardwood floor, a spectacular view, or a unique skylight, other liabilities such as size or location can be tolerated more easily. In decorating and personalizing this room or apartment, capitalize on its assets.

This small second-floor room has a wonderful old fireplace to provide cozy romantic moments for those who live here. A bed shaped with rolled-up ends similar to the scrolled front and back of an old-fashioned sleigh, minimizes the bedroom look. The matching armchair and footstool suggest that this room can also be used for reading or just relaxing before the fire.

Two windows have been treated in two different and distinct manners. The small window in the alcove behind the fireplace is covered with a straight panel, similar to a shade but drawn back by one corner to let in a little light. The diminutive and secluded character of the alcove is maintained by the illusion that the light has crept in through the half-opened curtain. The larger window on the other side of the fireplace is treated with a traverse curtain. Both curtains are made from material matching the wallpaper, which is again repeated in the mattress for accent. The orange of the armchair and stool provides a warm color complement to the striped walls.

As seen here, a room with a fireplace as the central focal point does not have to be lavishly furnished. A spare look actually highlights the fireplace. Following this example, if you don't want to buy a lot of furniture for a temporary home, invest in two or three quality pieces, and let the natural assets of the room speak for themselves.

*I*f you have to create a bedroom in a large loft-type space, you don't have to design an area that says nothing but "bedroom." About the only unavoidable bedroom element is the bed itself. In this room the bed blends right into what feels as much like a sitting room or living room as it does a bedroom.

A partition behind the bed conceals bureaus, clothes rack, changing area, and makeup table. Covered with fabrics that match others in the room, the pseudo-wall looks as substantial and permanent as the windows or built-in alcoves. By back-lighting the partition and allowing a leafy green ficus tree to peek up over it, one can almost imagine the arrangement was decided upon for aesthetic reasons alone.

Soft green and blue hues close to each other in the color range give this room a tight harmony that is restful and easy on the eye. The color scheme is faithfully followed in all areas of the room. Particularly stunning is the unusual window treatment. The blue fabric trims the two casements, gathered gracefully but not symmetrically across the top and hanging in full, lush folds down each side. The effect is to unite the two windows as one large one. A sheer green panel trimmed with material matching the comforter is hung in the lower half of each window for privacy and to adjust the intensity of light. When pulled back at one corner, pools of sunlight play across the room at odd angles, sweeping across the rug at the foot of the bed. The rug is a harmony of the warm colors, and its jaunty angle draws the eye away from the bed and to the comfortable chair and glass-topped table. The end result suggests that this is not a bedroom at all, but a cheery sitting room which happens to contain a bed.

*H*ere is an eclectic mix of furniture and decorative pieces tied together by color and pattern. The slats in the grey floor form the background of the room's design, carried onto the wall by the grey and white quilt, and complemented by the grey sofa. The variagated throw rug awakens the room while staying in synch with the slatted pattern of the floor, and it introduces the accent colors carried forward in the pillows on the sofa. The room's design extends into the bedroom by the progression of black accents, from the wing chair, to the pillows on the sofa, to the torchere lamp, and finally to the bed-side table. The eye travels from the red bedspread back to the red in the throw rug on the floor, tying the two rooms together beautifully.

One of the virtues of this room is the flexibility and open feeling of all the pieces of furniture and their arrangement. The two glass-topped tables are particularly appropriate, for they enhance the atmosphere of freedom and flexibility. The popsicle-stick-legged table works especially effectively to complement the room. It reflects the quilt from off the wall, but lets the colorful rug shine through, also.

*T*here is a disarming simplicity in this room that offers several useful decorating ideas for similar rooms dominated by a floor design either too imposing to ignore or too interesting to cover up. A black-and-white checkerboard pattern determines certain parameters in terms of color and geometric design and becomes a starting point for additional furnishings.

First, choose one color as a signature. In this case, pink offsets the two-color dominance. Pillows, a poster with just a center spot of pink in it, and a hobbyhorse with a pink saddle create the impression that there is just as much pink in this room as there is black and white.

Any other bright, bold color would have a similar effect.

Next, use the squared-off geometric pattern incorporated into the arrangement of furniture. The couch, the square coffee table, and the two large pillows on the floor create a rigid linear balance to the rows of alternating black and white squares. The staircase to the loft at the left reflects the checkerboard. Even the high-tech floor lamp by the couch rises to a right angle.

Yet, just as the pink accessories break up the rigidity of the two-color scheme, the plants and the hobbyhorse here interfere visually with the overwhelming geometry of the room. Imagine the room without them. It

would be completely dominated by right angles and symmetrical balance, an environment suggesting total control by the rational mind. The two gangling plants growing in their own directions, however, are objects of uncontrolled design with a life of their own. The hobbyhorse, in addition to introducing a symbol of animal vitality, suggests the restless playfulness of childhood, reminiscent of an age when spontaneity, fantasy, and whim were the important determinants. In this way, two or three objects carefully selected to offset the dominant look of a room are all that is needed to add variety and create a more interesting environment.

*H*ere is a long, narrow, open space personalized by a blend of the casual and the elegant, the simple and the complex. Artistic refinement, expressed in royal reds and purples, contrasts casually with weathered and worn floorboards. The framed and unframed canvases leaning against the wall refute the traditional method of display, but their playful pastel colors mix well with the sedate deep reds, purples, and blacks in the rest of the furnishings, so they fit easily into the decorating scheme. In fact, the abstractions rendered upon them provide relief to the complexity of the hanging prints and the rich rugs.

The length of the room itself is visually tempered by its careful division into three distinct spaces. In the foreground is the living room, outlined by chairs and sofa on three sides and the coffee table and pendant brass light fixture on the fourth. The dining room becomes an easily recognizable sibling to the living room by the rug of similar color tones and size. The two rooms are also visually joined by the run of ornate arabesque wall hangings that extend up to the kitchen in the background. Yet even the kitchen is a not-too-distant cousin to the first two rooms. The easy-going cluttered look of the open shelves and the utensils and pictures mounted on the wall echoes the nonchalance of the unframed canvases leaning against the wall in the living room. From area to area, this space embodies carefully designed haphazardness. Furthermore, although it seems complicated and rather permanent in its design, every element can easily be transferred to the next home.

*T*he images of an exciting safari theme used by the designer of this playful room create a comfortable yet austere environment, uniting the adventure of an exotic continent with the amenities of a modern Western living room. The brighter colors in the room stand out against the basic desert sand color of the background walls, furniture, and carpet, much as they would in direct sunlight. Two types of accent colors are used against the neutral sand: muted greens and pinks in the carpet design, and bold swatches of red and yellow whisked like parrot feathers on the painting over the couch. Elephants, flamingos, and lions contribute a whimsical yet unobtrusive menagerie effect on the floor, with the satin accent pillows on the couch echoing the carpet's soft colors. The

dark leafiness of the potted palms and the bright flowers used as decorative highlights enhance the jungle effect.

Notice that the clear glass-topped coffee table almost disappears visually—a perfect piece of furniture to prevent a tight, crowded look and maintain the spaciousness in keeping with the safari motif. A baby spotlight is aimed to emphasize the spectacular colors of the painting on the wall and the candles and plants along the shelf behind the couch. Decorative items are displayed in a simple yet tasteful manner on the single shelf behind the couch, eliminating added clutter from shelves built on a bare wall or space taken up by another table. In tight quarters, the space behind the couch and under the shelf can be used for storage.

*A*s the selection of electronic media for home use increases, we are confronted with a new decorating challenge. The basic question is where do you store and use the new equipment when you do not have a separate media room or even a media corner. Future homes may be designed with special rooms for the new technology, but until that day arrives we'll have to be content with jerry-rigging equipment wherever we can—a word processor in the kitchen, a sound system in the living room, and a television in the bedroom.

In this room, technology is introduced as a definite design statement by giving it a place of preeminence. The modular desk unit serves as a headboard for the bed and divides the room into sleeping section and office section. The desk also functions as a command module for operating radio, television, and other media that can be hooked up to it.

Because this room is small, a choice was made not to place the television on the floor and detract from the fireplace but to mount it on the wall above the fireplace. Now the occupant can enjoy both fireplace and television. Other high-tech touches are the two reading lamps, one by the bed and the other near the lounge chair by the window. Metal blinds complete the high-tech look.

In spite of using technology as a decorative motif for the room, there is still place for more traditional objects to complement the lovely fireplace. A sculpted Oriental head on the mantel and classical columns that frame the window are reminiscent of earlier eras. The columns can be made from any material (heavy cardboard cylinders would work fine). Stretch fabric around them tightly and bridge them at the top with a swag of the same material gathered into graceful folds.

# SOURCES/USEFUL ADDRESSES

## CRAMPED QUARTERS

**Charles Giulioli**
60 Lispenard St.
New York, NY 10013

**Krueger**
P.O. Box 8100
Green Bay, WI 54308

**Rangine Corp.**
114 Union St.
Millis, MA 02054

**Shoji Workshop**
21-10 31st Ave.
Astoria, NY 11106

**Taylor Woodcraft**
P.O. Box 245
South River Rd.
Malta, OH 43758

## SPARSE STORAGE

**Amerock Corp.**
P.O. Box 7018
4000 Auburn St.
Rockford, IL 61125

**Charmglow Products**
P.O. Box 127
Bristol, WI 53104

**Clairson/
Closet Maid**
720 S.W. 17th St.
Ocala, FL 36270

**Ikea**
1224 Dundas St.
Toronto, ONT L4Y 2C1

**Inter Metro Industries**
North Washington St.
Wilkes-Barre, PA 18705

## SECURITY

**Brookstone**
648 Vose Farm Rd.
Peterborough, NH 03458

**City Wide
Locksmiths**
1750 Avenue Road S.
Toronto, ONT M5M 3Y9

**Honeywell, Inc.**
9900 Bren Road E.
Minneapolis, MN 55343

**Medeco Security Locks, Inc.**
P.O. Box 1075
Salem, VA 24153

**Mountain West**
4215 N. 16th St.
P.O. Box 10780
Phoenix, AZ 85064

**Schlage**
2401 Bayshore Blvd.
San Francisco, CA 94134

**Tools for Living**
205 Liberty Sq.
Norwalk, CT 06855

## A COMFORTABLE CLIMATE

**Fedders Air Conditioning**
415 Wabash Ave.
Effingham, IL 62401

**Gracious Home**
1220 3rd Ave.
New York, NY 10021

**York
Air Conditioning**
1188 Martingrove
Rexdale, ONT M9W 5M9

## WALLS, FLOORS, CEILING

**Apartment Painting
Service**
11A Boston
Toronto, ONT M 4M 2T8

**B.B. Bargoons**
199 Queen St. E.
Toronto, ONT M5A 1S2

**Charles Barone Inc.**
9505 W. Jefferson
Culver City, CA 90232

**Country Curtains**
at the Red Lion Inn
Stockbridge, MA 01262

**Dellinger Inc.**
1943 N. Broad
Rome, GA 30161

**Flooring Ltd.**
149 Norfinch Dr.
Toronto, ONT M3N 1Y2

**Laura Ashley**
714 Madison Ave.
New York, NY 10021

**Marimekko Inc.**
1 Dock St.
Stamford, CT 06902

**Mirror Graphics**
275 Andrews Rd.
Mineola, NY 11501

**Routleys**
1640 Avenue Rd.
Toronto, ONT M5M 3X9

**St. Clair**
218 Young St.
Toronto Eaton Centre
Toronto, ONT M5B 286

**Summitville Tile**
Dept. K & BB
Summitville, OH 43962

**Warner
Wallcoverings & Fabrics**
108 S. Desplaines St.
Chicago, IL 60606

**Woodson**
200 Lexington Ave.
New York, NY 10016

## WINDOWS

**Gardisette**
P.O. Box 2586
Anderson, SC 29622

**Home and Castle Inc.**
20941 Roscoe Blvd.
Canoga Park, CA 91304

**Levolor Lorentzen Inc.**
1280 Wall St. W.
Lyndhurst, NJ 07071

**Pinecrest**
2118 Blaisdell Ave.
Minneapolis, MN 55404

**Rue de France**
78 Thames St.
Newport, RI 02840

## LIGHTING

**Artemide**
150 E. 58th St.
New York, NY 10155

**Eleusi**
Via Giuseppe Verdi, 7
Casella Postale 21, Italy

**Lighting Associates, Inc.**
305 E. 63rd St.
New York, NY 10021

**Nessen Lamps**
3200 Jerome Ave.
Bronx, NY 10468

**Traklite Inc.**
Troy Lighting Co.
14625 E. Clark Ave.
City of Industry, CA 91746

## COLLECTIONS

**Botanix**
10 State St.
Moonachie, NY 07074

**Fuller Office Furniture Corp.**
45 E. 57th St.
New York, NY 10022

**Nevins Worldwide**
4342 W. 12th St.
Houston, TX 77055

**Vemaline Products**
487 Jefferson Blvd.
Warwick, RI 02886

## KITCHEN & BATHROOM

**Artistic Brass**
4100 Ardmore Ave.
South Gate, CA 90280

**Dura Supreme**
10750 County Rd. 15
Minneapolis, MN 55441

**Franke Inc.**
Kitchen Systems Division
212 Church Rd.
North Wales, PA 19454

**Hafele**
P.O. Box 1590
203 Feld Ave.
High Point, NC 27261

**Iron-A-Way**
220 W. Jackson
Morton, IL 61550

**Poggenpohl U.S.A. Corp.**
6 Pearl Ct.
Allendale, NJ 07401

**Sherle Wagner, Inc.**
60 E. 57th St.
New York, NY 10022

**Villeroy & Boch Inc.**
P.O. Box 103
Pine Brook, NJ 07058

**Wilardy**
2600 N. Pulaski Rd.
Chicago, IL 60639

## FURNITURE

**Amisco**
C.P. 250
L'Islet, QUE G0R 2C0

**The Art Shoppe**
2131 Yonge St.
Toronto, ONT M4S 2A7

**Atelier International**
595 Madison Ave.
New York, NY 10022

**De Boers**
5051 Yonge St.
Toronto, ONT M2N 5P2

**Futon Company**
10-12 Rivington St.
London, ENG EC2

**Kartell U.S.A.**
225 Fifth Ave.
New York, NY 10010

**Level of Winchendon**
28 Front St.
Winchendon, MA 01457

**Paoli Chair Co.**
P.O. Box 30
Paoli, IN 47454

**Roche-Bobois U.S.A. Ltd.**
200 Madison Ave.
New York, NY 10016

**Spatial Environmental Elements**
118 Spring St.
New York, NY 10012

**Waddingtons**
189 Queen St. E.
Toronto, ONT M5A 1S2

**The Workbench**
470 Park Ave. S.
New York, NY 10016

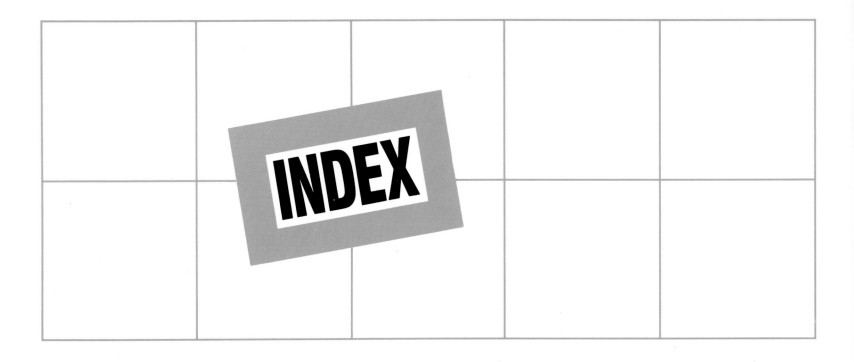

# PICTURE CREDITS

**Amerock:** 49(r), 114
**Amisco:** 25(t)
**Artemide:** 98, 100(l), 104, 107
**Bieffeplast:** 99
**Bouchet, Guy; Kim Freeman** (stylist): 21(t), 63, 88(b)
**Brookstone:** 53(tl), 53(bl)
**Charmglow:** 36
**Chowanetz, Gary/EWA:** 15
**Cripps, David/EWA:** 32
**Davis, Richard/EWA:** 30, 62
**Derrick and Love:** 33(t), 72
**Dunne, Michael/EWA:** 73, 96, 117(br), 111, 144–145, 151(br)
**Eleusi:** 102(b)
**Ennis, Phillip H:** 16(b), 84(1), 127
**French, John:** 79(tl)
**Futon Co., London:** 26(b), 143
**General Electric:** 53(tr)
**Giovanni, Raeanne; Kim Freeman** (stylist): 91(r)
**Giulioli, Charles:** 97
**Graham, Boyce:** 124(l)
**Helm, Clive/EWA:** 67
**Henderson, Graham/EWA:** 90
**Honeywell:** 47(t), 50, 51
**Kartell, U.S.A.:** 10, 14(r), 43(b), 45(r)
**Krause, Rainer; Courtesy of Peter Frank:** 35(r), 77
NR/Photographer
**Laura Ashley:** 19(br), 129(r), 146
**Levin, James R.:** 12(b), 16(t), 22, 26(t), 30(t), 31, 38(l), 40, 41(t), 42(r), 66(t), 70(l), 74(b), 83(bl), 85, 94, 112(l), 122, 123(b), 147

**Levin, Robert:** 73(b)
**Levolor Lorentzen, Inc.:** 11(b), 89, 90, 152
**Maison Designs:** 128(t)
**Medeco Co.:** 48
**Motif:** 81, 92
**Mountain West:** 50–51
**Nieman, Julian/EWA:** 113(bl)
**Nicholson, Mike/EWA:** 135, 138
**O'Rourke, Randy:** 30(br), 71, 75, 103(b), 116, 119(t), 144
**Paige, Peter:** 101(b), 106, 149
**Poggenpohl:** 44(l), 70(r), 123(t)
**Powell, Spike/EWA:** 139
**Pinecrest:** 84(r), 95(l)
**Roche Bobois:** 12–13, 20(r), 43(t), 45(l), 71, 105
**Ross, Richard:** 33(b), 126(b)
**Rothchild, Bill, Carole Price** (designer): 88(tl)
**Rue de France:** 88–89
**Schenck, Gordon:** 58, 129(l)
**Schwartz, John** (for Westchester Custom Kitchens): 56(b), 59, 121; (for Miles J. Lourie): 78, 112(r)
**Spatial Environmental Elements:** 34 (photo: Esto Peter Mauss)
**Street-Porter, Tim:** 9, 11(r), 24, 27, 66(b), 87, 102(t), 117(t); **EWA:** 15, 68, 93, 100(r)
**Taylor Woodcraft, Inc.:** 28, 29(b)
**Tools for Living:** 47(b), 52
**Trakliting:** 55(r), 109
**Weiss, Jeffery:** 41(b), 49(l), 54, 55(l), 56(t), 57, 60, 76, 79(bl), 79(br), 86, 110, 134, 136, 137, 150
**Workbench:** 14(l), 42(l)

**KEY TO ILLUSTRATION CODES:**
*tl:* top left; *tc:* top center; *tr:* top right; *cl:* center left; *cc:* center center; *cr:* center right; *bl:* bottom left; *bc:* bottom center; *br:* bottom right; *t:* top; *c:* center; *b:* bottom; *l:* left; *r:* right